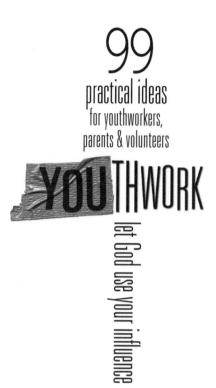

99 practical ideas for youthworkers, parents & volunteers

YOUTHWORK

let God use your influence

DON PEARSON & PAUL SANTHOUSE

MOODY PUBLISHERS
CHICAGO

To Louie Konopka, who for twenty-seven years has been my lead pastor, friend, and mentor. It's one thing to be told how to do life; quite another to be shown.

— Don

To Rebecca, Rachel, Jonathan & Amy, Sarah, Jacob, and Anneliese. I am blessed above all men.

— Paul

All Scripture quotations, unless otherwise indicated, are taken from the *Holy Bible, New International Version®*. NIV®. Copyright © 1973, 1978, 1984 by International Bible Society. Used by permission of Zondervan. All rights reserved.

Scripture quotations marked MSG are from *The Message*, copyright © 1993, 1994, 1995 by Eugene Peterson. Used by permission of NavPress Publishing Group.

Scripture quotations marked NASB are taken from the *New American Standard Bible®*. Copyright © 1960, 1962, 1963, 1968, 1971, 1972, 1973, 1975, 1977, 1995 by The Lockman Foundation. Used by permission (www.Lockman.org)

Editor: Randall J. Payleitner
Interior and Cover Design: Julia Ryan/www.DesignByJulia.com
Cover Images: ©2009 iStock.com

ISBN: 978-0-8024-0970-6

Pearson, Don.
Youthwork– let God use your influence : 99 practical ideas for youthworkers, parents, and volunteers / Don Pearson and Paul Santhouse.
p. cm.
Includes bibliographical references.
ISBN 978-0-8024-0970-6
1. Church work with youth. I. Santhouse, Paul. II. Title.
BV4447.P35 2009
259'.23–dc22
2009008583

This book is printed on acid free recycled paper containing 30% PCW (Post Consumer Waste) and manufactured in the United States of America by Bethany Press.

We hope you enjoy this book from Moody Publishers. Our goal is to provide high-quality, thought-provoking books and products that connect truth to your real needs and challenges. For more information on other books and products written and produced from a biblical perspective, go to www.moodypublishers.com or write to:

Moody Publishers
820 N. LaSalle Boulevard
Chicago, IL 60610

1 3 5 7 9 10 8 6 4 2

Printed in the United States of America

Contents

In the Beginning

in the **beginning**

June 1, 1987
Poor Mark.

After months of hype about launching a new youth program, Mark was finally getting what he'd dreamed of—a youth group! Friends. Adventures. A place to belong. *Finally.*

There was just one problem: of the five kids on the roster, four didn't show up. I'll never forget the look on Mark's face the night of our first big event. It seems the other kids had made other plans. Plans that didn't include Mark or our dorky youth group. So Mark hung out with my wife and me at McDonald's. Two volunteers and one student. Some youth group . . .

June 1, many years later . . .
Lucky Kyle (Mark's nephew).

He's finally reached high school and there are six hundred students in his group. He's waited years for this summer, saving money and debating trip options with friends. He chose two—a sailing adventure called "Dawntreader" and a Mexico mission trip. "Dawntreader" threw him together with two hundred others on eighteen sailboats up in the North Channel of Lake Huron. And

Mexico brought him face-to-face with hundreds of poor, Spanish-speaking children. They swarmed around him while he dug holes, poured concrete, ate weird food, and got diarrhea. He loved every minute of it.

During the forty-hour ride home he dreamed of coming back next year. He also thought about the possibility of a wilderness trip. Tetons or Glacier? But that choice would have to wait—there was too much to think about before then. Like his upcoming small group and how he hoped they'd become some of his best friends this year. In fact, one of his buddies from school, a guy he'd been praying for since seventh grade, had recently agreed to join. How cool was that? *I guess prayer does work,* he thought on his way to the bathroom . . .

"Lucky"

In the beginning there was Mark. Now there are over six hundred students in fifty small groups, two hundred adult volunteers, ten paid youth staff, two hundred and eighty athletes in a basketball outreach league, three coach buses (two of which currently have full waste tanks waiting to be emptied), a bike trailer that holds one hundred chain-driven insurance hazards, and over a thousand trips, retreats, and events on the record books. Our mission teams have preached Christ and pounded nails in other countries, and several students have returned to those same countries for longer visits after graduating.

Who was luckier? Mark or Kyle?

Well, neither—it's a trick question. Both were blessed to have people like *you* investing in their lives. Students can thrive in any setting. Mark flourished as "The Lone Student." His enthusiasm for our "group" was so contagious the younger kids begged to join. And Kyle's group threw off a ton of energy. Kids showed up just to feel like they were a part of something. So it's not the size or scope of your work that counts. It's the fact that you're influencing the kids God gave you. That's what matters.

Few things get me more excited than helping young people encounter Jesus Christ. That's what drew me back in the early eighties when my wife and I started volunteering, and it's what keeps me going today. It's also why I put this book together. There are millions of students out there waiting for someone to participate in their spiritual journey. Someone like you.

Tools of the trade

The best ideas almost always come from experience. And life is too short to gather all that experience yourself. I've learned plenty in the decades I've been doing this, but I've borrowed even more from others. This book combines the best of both worlds —homegrown insights refined through trial and error and great ideas adapted from others that bear fruit every time we use them.

Whether you are working with youth right now or you plan to someday, keep on reading. It doesn't matter if you're full-time, part-time, paid, volunteer, a parent, or a student. Our team is made up of all the above, and we all gain momentum from the insights packed into these pages. Every point in the journey can add some major value: from nurturing spiritual maturity to planning life-changing trips.

If you're like me, you'll be able to scan these pages and spot twenty ideas that will help you and your students *right now*. So give yourself some time, grab a pencil, and come up with a plan using some of the ideas in the following pages. Then watch God multiply your love for the students in your life. ●

invest

THE last guy I ever expected to see in my youth group was Mr. Jenkins. He wasn't the type. Pushing sixty, hard of hearing, and always in a suit. Imagine my surprise when he barged into our group one night and loudly introduced us to his "buddy," a long-haired boy named Tom.

Now the town I grew up in was a small town where people knew each other. That's why we stared at Mr. Jenkins when he showed up with Tom. We recognized Tom from school. He was one of "those kids." What's he doing here? I wondered as they found their seats. True to form, Mr. Jenkins sat ramrod-straight in a folding chair while Tom sprawled across a couch. His clothing reeked of marijuana and his shaggy hair fell all over his shoulders—and in our conservative church I wasn't sure which was worse. Tom had been hitch-hiking when Mr. Jenkins picked him up, and it looked like he was still not sure where he was.

Few of us paid attention to the lesson that night—we were all watching Tom. But Mr. Jenkins was taking every-thing in. His wheels were turning and his lips were moving in (almost) silent prayer for Tom's salvation.

Remarkably, the two of them became friends. Mr. Jenkins gave Tom an enormous brown Bible, and Tom carried it everywhere. Over time we welcomed him into our community, and one day he came into relationship with Jesus Christ. Just like that.

That's when I learned a lesson I'll never forget: God uses ordinary people to draw youth to Himself. *No ministry degrees required and no special gifting necessary. Anyone will do.*

 You are qualified

Obviously, some people are gifted. They can't cross the parking lot without a trail of kids following in their wake. But if you are not one of those, fear not. Youthwork has many entry points besides gifting. For example:

- **A burden.** God has placed certain young people on your heart. Whether it's the babysitter or the kid next door, their names clutter your prayers because of their obvious need for Christ.

- **The asset of time.** Scheduling a meal with a young person or attending a youth retreat doesn't set you back at all. You have margin to give.

- **The ability to listen.** Like us, young people long to be cared about. By making eye contact and showing an interest in what they're thinking, feeling, and doing, you demonstrate the kind of care that invites relationship.

- **A loving heart.** Love knows no opposition and melts the hardest heart. What more needs to be said?

The bottom line is this—whether you're a parent, a paid youth-worker, or a volunteer, God can use you to shepherd students. I've been watching it happen for nearly three decades.

2 A two-question test

It's not uncommon for adults to view students as a different species. They look different, act different, dress different, talk different, relate different, listen to different music . . . and appear disinterested. Join a cluster of students and watch how quickly they stop talking or fade away. No wonder so many adults feel they have nothing to offer and no place to start. Awkwardness and rejection don't top my list of favorite experiences either. Have you ever felt this way?

It's important to remember that appearances don't represent reality when it comes to investing in young people. You have more to offer than you realize. Just ask yourself two questions:

Question One: *Can I remember what it was like to be an adolescent?*

Not *do* you remember, but *can* you remember. You may not have thought about it for years, but, if you try, can you remember? Can you recall looking for a place to sit in the cafeteria? The social positioning at football games and special events? Sitting in class and being so absorbed with a romantic crush the teacher's words seemed a distant droning? Can you remember the dreams? Scoring the winning basket, rescuing the girl in distress, hoping a certain someone would ask you to homecoming, voicing the perfect comeback, or achieving the honor of being named valedictorian? Were you ever embarrassed beyond words by something you did, or shamed by something that happened to you? Was your world ever shattered by relational treachery? Were you ever in ecstasy because of a "perfect encounter" with the person you adored? How about this—do you remember a time when God was at work in your heart, stirring your soul, seemingly close enough to touch? If you can remember any of these things or how you felt at the time, you remember what it was like to be an adolescent. You can relate.

Question Two: *Are there any aspects of my life worth imitating?*

We're not talking about perfection here. Remember, the love of Christ is radical because it meets us where we are, not where we should be. *Young people need steps to climb, not cliffs to scale.* Can you recognize any growth in your character over the past several years? How about since you were in middle school? Are you making any progress in knowing God? In recognizing His ways? Have you experienced growth in your prayer life or understanding of Scripture since high school?

Answering *yes* to these two main questions is more basic to youthwork than earning five degrees. Why? Because empathizing with students and offering them a window into the character of God is central to helping them follow Christ.

3 There's a secret to Steve's coolness

We go to a conference every year where five thousand youthworkers gather for growth and encouragement. At the beginning of the conference they have everyone stand up who has been in youth work five years or more. Then they say, "Remain standing if you've been at it for ten years." They keep this up until just three or four are standing in the entire hall. Then they ask each one, "Tell us, how long have you been working with youth?"

Invariably, those still standing are humble, grey-haired veterans who quietly utter, "Oh, forty or fifty years."

These are the heroes. They are the unsung legends of youth ministry who were working with their own kids or investing in others long before "youthwork" was even a recognized occupation. They discovered it doesn't matter how old you are, what you wear, or if you're up on the latest music or movies. What matters is that you have an authentic walk with God and that you care about the young people in your world.

Youthwork, like parenting, is more about what's caught than what's taught. Can't you just hear a middle school student saying something like this?

Steve is cool . . .

Steve loves God . . .

Me too. I love God too.

So here's the million dollar question: *What makes Steve so cool?* Is he wearing the right stuff? Listening to the right music? Using the right words? Why is Steve bigger than life to this kid?

Because he loves the kid.

How else can you explain what happened between Mr. Jenkins and Tom? Mr. Jenkins had always been invisible to us, probably because we felt invisible to him. The same held true for Tom. We never gave him a passing thought, except to condemn him when we needed an ego boost. But love changed everything. Mr. Jenkins became a respected fixture in our youth group. Tom became a believer *and* an evangelist. And the rest of us learned to bring Christ to the kids at school rather than focusing on our own cliques and interests. In fact, the trickle-down from that Wednesday night surprise included my own decision to enter youth ministry, a calling I'm still engaged in several decades later.

"Follow me as I follow Christ"

Let's say there is a girl in your youth group named Andrea and she has an eating disorder. Does she need professional help? Yes. Especially if she's in immediate danger. But, in addition to making sure her short-term needs are met, don't forget about her long-term need. Like all of us, Andrea's thinking needs to be rooted in truth. Does Andrea have value and worth as a person? Is she loved? Do others need what only she can bring into their lives? Does she have something to live for? Yes to all of these and more. If Andrea can learn to walk in truth, she will begin to see things through their proper lenses.

The trouble is, we spend half of our lives creating our own truth. We believe we are unwanted, unlovable, unworthy. Our lives don't matter, and our contributions make no difference. It doesn't seem like anyone cares, and why should they? Our experience in a broken world confirms these thoughts and so we convince ourselves they are true in order to justify our behavior.

So why can't we line all the kids up against the wall and tell them they're loved, valuable, and significant? Because that's not how beliefs form in the hearts of the young. Rather, they develop through the nurture of loving adults. Beliefs need to be seen, felt, double-checked, and tested. They need to hold up on good days and bad days. They can't be purchased from a medical examiner or a counseling expert. They don't come in nicely packaged, thirty-minute sessions.

Andrea has something few other teens have. She has a youth leader named Susie on her side. Susie is investing time and energy in Andrea's life. She has gained Andrea's trust, *and she has been a great listener.* As their lives intermingle over time, the younger watches the older like a hawk (though not always noticeably). Andrea's soul comes alive with hope as she hears stories of how Susie wrestles with her own body image. Susie is honest about how she processes the input of family, friends, and the media. And Susie is unabashed in sharing how she came to know *and trust* Jesus in the tender, shame-filled areas of her life.

Susie doesn't tell Andrea what to think. She demonstrates what's true. And over time a *transfer* takes place. What Susie believes transfers to Andrea. This is the sacred core of youthwork. *Follow me as I follow Christ.*

5 This sure does cost a lot . . .

It's 10:30 p.m. and I'm completely drained. My day was horrendous, both emotionally and physically. For the past two hours I've been fighting sleep, but I have a problem. My living room is littered with students.

Rachel and Amy are sprawled on the couch, their dialogue crackling with intensity. A blizzard could pass through the room and they wouldn't notice.

Jacob, Vince, and Jonathan are playing guitars in the corner and I'm amazed, yet again, at how effortless it seems for those guys to play their own original stuff. It's that good.

My greatest joy, however, is that Anneliese, Sarah, and Courtney are talking on the hearth. The fire must be frying their backs, but they seem oblivious. That means Courtney is now "in the group."

I'm tired, I'm old, and as I carry dishes to the kitchen I'm banging the glasses against each other in a feeble attempt to remind them that group ended an hour ago. But it's no use. This is a Wednesday thing. A secret club where stories are told. A real, live facebook. My wife and I wouldn't trade it for anything. This semester we're helping students discover the lies that lurk in the shadows of their soul, energizing poor choices. Their inward journeys are the stuff of high adventure. To watch them morph before our very eyes is what keeps a couple of old, tired youthworkers going. Chances are you know exactly what I mean. Or you soon will. ●

strategize

AFTER *two hours of wandering the dark neighborhood, Zach stopped at a house with a basketball hoop. Can't go back home, he told himself. So he curled up on the dew-soaked grass behind the hoop and shut his eyes.*

Years later he'd explain why he chose that yard to sleep in. The girl who lived there was nice to him at school. It was that simple. He knew she was a Christian, but overlooked it because she smiled at him. In those days smiles were rare.

Before falling asleep, he topped off his anger tank by replaying the events of the night. He recalled rushing home from his first job to mow the backyard, as his stepdad had ordered. He'd finished so quickly he managed to cut the front yard too before heading off to his second job . . . where he washed dishes for six straight hours in the steamy kitchen of the country club.

Riding home late that night he was surprised to see the front light on and the door open. That's strange, he thought. They're usually asleep by now.

When Zach spotted his stepdad standing on the sidewalk out front, he remembered having mowed the front yard. A warm feeling came over him as he realized his stepdad probably stayed up late to thank him.

Stepping off the moped he eagerly turned to meet the man's gaze . . . and froze. There was that look—the one he'd seen so many times these past six months.

Without even waiting for Zach to remove his helmet, his stepfather got right in his face and jabbed his finger toward the sidewalk. "What's this?" he demanded.

Zach looked where the finger pointed, searching in vain for some clue. With a blank stare he raised his eyes.

"Clippings," spat the man, adding choice words for emphasis. "If you want the privilege of mowing the front yard, try doing it right next time!" With that he spun around, entered the house, and slammed the door. A moment later the lights went out.

Zach stood there a long time, staring into the night. Then he set his helmet on the moped seat and started walking. And he never went back.

But he didn't disappear. He showed up at our youth group.

 Strategy is ministry

What would you have done with Zach? What's your plan for reaching kids like Zach with the gospel? How will you disciple them to maturity in Christ?

What about the others in your group? Not everyone walks in off the street. Some grow up in the church and seem healthy. Others are dragged in by their parents and resent you from the start. And then there are those who drift in and out, wounded by life and hungry for love. What's your plan for shepherding these kids?

I have two immediate thoughts every time our elders ask to see "my plan." First, *I hate paperwork.* If I liked paperwork I'd get an office job. All my business friends complain bitterly about strategic planning. Hours of time, reams of paper, and endless meetings. What a waste. When I showed up for my first day as a youthworker, the senior pastor called me into his office. "I don't want to see you in here," he said. "You belong with students and families, not behind a desk." I couldn't believe my ears! No plans, no reports, and no meetings—just pure ministry. I was out the door before he could change his mind.

What I didn't realize at the time was that *he* had a plan, and he'd just launched Phase One.

His plan turned out to be a good one, which leads to my second immediate thought when asked for a plan—*it's crucial to have one*. When you're working with youth, you need a clear vision of what seventh graders should look like in six short years. And you must know how to get them there. Not to know these things is to waste everyone's time.

No, it's worse than that. It's to squander incalculable opportunity. Crafting a functional strategy is the key to making a difference. And creating this strategy is pure ministry.

7 Spiritual work requires spiritual strength

Some strategic plans are so brilliant they'll work no matter who executes them. At least for a while. But genius only goes so far. The same with giftedness, charm, and drive. Ultimately you need spiritual strength to do spiritual work.

"I am the vine; you are the branches. If a man remains in me and I in him, he will bear much fruit; apart from me you can do nothing" (John 15:5). That's what Jesus said, and that's exactly how it works. It's one thing to run dry every so often—happens to all of us. But to carry on a spiritual enterprise without the Spirit is like running a restaurant without food.

So how does a youthworker *abide?* You'll need to craft your own specifics, but I can guarantee a few nonnegotiables. The Word is invaluable. It makes faith possible. It clarifies God's priorities and showcases His sovereignty. Jesus' ministry is rich with insight and example. Narrative passages add flesh and bones to theory, making it clear how to follow His lead. The Prophets demonstrate how God feels about sin, and the Psalms express His love for sinners. Stay in the Word. Long-term youthwork is impossible without it.

The same is true for prayer. It's how we partner with God in His business of redeeming lives. Discuss everything with Him. Talk about students, review plans, check motives, and surrender control. Beg Him for results, cry out to Him for your family, and plead with Him for the lost. The more you pray, the better you see through His lens and depend on His grace. The blood and guts of youthwork is in prayer. Ministry with students is just the fruit.

A buddy of mine told me about his experience as a human sump pump. When a severe storm left him without power for two full days, he had water overflowing his sump hole at the rate of one gallon per minute. That calculates to more than 2,500 gallons of water. Which means more than five hundred trips up from the basement, out the back door, and over the deck railing with a five-gallon pail. Twenty-four hours a day. For two straight days. On the morning of the second day his wife observed that doing the work of a sump pump without electricity is like doing ministry without the Holy Spirit. Amen to that! (She also observed it might be nice to own a generator . . .)

The average life consists of 25,550 days. Most of them contain enough frenzy, pressure, expectations, distractions, and self-centeredness to squeeze your relationship with God down to the size of a raisin. But remember: *your work with students will follow your connection to God.*

 ## 8 Build a pyramid

On a recent trip to Mexico with our graduating seniors, we scaled an ancient pyramid. It was mammoth, and we were crawling on hands and knees by the time we reached the top. Not every visitor makes the climb, and not all who attempt it reach the top (which is good because there wasn't much room up there).

According to veteran youthworker Dann Spader, Jesus' ministry experience followed the same pattern as our trek up the pyramid. Though He met people where they were and offered something more to each of them, not all responded the same way. There were crowds who heard, disciples who listened, twelve who followed, and three who were intimate. In each case Christ met them where they were and offered something more.

After observing this pattern in the Gospels, Dann organized his youth ministry around it. Not all the students in his church were interested in following Christ. Among those who did wish to follow, some longed for a deeper relationship, and a few aspired to spiritual maturity and leadership. The group was wide at the base and narrow at the top.

Many youth programs target the top groups—those hungry for serious growth or leadership. Jesus, on the other hand, cried, "Come to me, all you who are weary and burdened, and I will give you rest" (Matthew 11:28).

Some approach this concept as a choice between evangelism and discipleship—preferring one or the other. But the beauty of strategic planning is that you can insert as many levels into your pyramid as you'd like. Here's what our pyramid looks like:

Leadership (come and
lead other students)

Ministry (come and serve)

Growth (come and learn)

Outreach (come and hear the gospel)

Relational (come and build friendships)

Think back to the story of Zach (at the beginning of this chapter). He didn't come in the door looking for God, yet he emerged spiritually changed. God used what we had in place to move him from off the radar to off the charts. He knew the Bible in about six months and believed every word of it. Every month he'd show up with five pages of questions drawn from his personal Bible study. It amazes me to reflect on how God used His Word to change that boy, and how He allowed our group to serve as a stepping-stone in the process. Keep examples like this in mind as you strategize your model.

Not all events have the same goal

Students are remarkably diverse, and they each represent varying stages of interest. Keep this in mind as you build your strategy. Your events, trips, groups, and lessons can be targeted and tailored to the pyramid level you're attempting to reach. Imagine being able to answer *yes* to each of the following criticisms:

- **Do you mean to tell me you hosted an entire event and never taught from the Bible?** (Yes! We're reaching out to a new group of students who have no interest in faith at this time. This event was designed to build bridges and there were subsequent activities lined up to introduce them to Jesus Christ.)

- **Do I understand correctly that my son was not allowed to attend his small group on Monday night?** (Yes! The purpose of the group is spiritual growth, and since he's not interested either in growth or even regular attendance at this time, his occasional appearances were actually disrupting the other students.)

- **My daughter informed me that no one showered the entire week of your Mexico trip. Is this true?** (Yes! There was no water available for showering. And since our goal was to serve, not to primp, everyone accepted this condition as part of the cost of making a difference.)

- **Do I understand correctly that you are using half your annual budget on 5 percent of the students?** (Yes! We've placed a high priority on leadership development this year because good leaders benefit the students, and we don't have enough of them lined up to get us through the next several years.)

Each of these situations might seem outrageous until you consider the pyramid tier we're working with (note the different goals between the following two tiers):

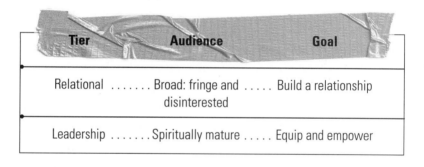

Tier	Audience	Goal
Relational	Broad: fringe and disinterested	Build a relationship
Leadership	Spiritually mature	Equip and empower

Making decisions based on a pyramid model will help you plan the best opportunities to reach, nurture, and train a wide variety of students. Like the ones in your church.

10 Maybe the most important thing

I keep Hebrews 10:14 near the top of my mental desk: "Because by one sacrifice he has made perfect forever those who are being made holy." In one verse I'm reminded how God views our students. He sees their perfection. He shed blood to make them perfect.

They're also messy. Not yet holy. They struggle. They learn things but don't live them. In short, they're being sanctified.

Your students will delight, distress, challenge, and frustrate you. But God loves them completely. That's why He entrusted them to your care. Keep this in mind and it will keep you going for the long haul.

 ## 11 Look for the world-changers

When Stuart was in seventh grade you could barely spot it, but it was there. Maybe not while he was belching in Sunday school but if you studied him long enough you'd recognize the signs. He was a world-changer. An influencer. *A natural leader.* If you could keep Stuart interested, you held the entire group in your hands.

What do you want Stuart to look like when he graduates from your program? Where do you want him leading others? Sketch a mental picture for yourself. Get as specific as you can. Describe the "future Stuart" as *The New York Times* would profile a statesman.

Sonlife Ministries calls this a "Description of a Discipled Person," or DDP. In their DDP, they list essential skills, attitudes, and knowledge that a person should obtain during the years they spend in your programs.

If you can, make one for each specific student. It will bring your values into sharp focus. The more time you spend working this out, the more you'll understand your students, what Scripture they know, how they use it, and the difference it makes in their lives.

 ## 12 Keep it simple

Few decisions in life are major. Most are just steps along a path. What matters is the path. Those who win trophies and those who commit crimes don't typically wake up in the morning and decide that's what they'll do that day. They get up and walk their path, making decisions along the way.

Your strategic plan is your path.

Near the end of last year we evaluated our expenditures. Every one of us voiced concern over the money we were spending on student trips. As a result, we shifted a large slice of next year's budget to a different area.

That decision—involving tens of thousands of dollars—was easy to make. Our strategic plan called for one outcome, and our spending patterns pointed to another. So we retooled the budget. No politics and no remorse. (Well, there was *some* remorse, but no one mounted a hunger strike.)

The genius of strategic planning is that it helps you make decisions . . . as long as you keep it simple. You should be able to explain it to a dad over fast food or to the elders in ten minutes. And you should see heads nodding while you talk.

Jesus was a master at this: "I am the bread of life . . . I am the Vine; you are the branches . . . I will make you fishers of men . . . A farmer was scattering seed." And so on.

The other benefit of simplicity is that *you* remember what you're doing. When the school year kicks in and your calendar becomes a blur, you want something you can recite in the car between appointments. Something that keeps you focused and reminds you why you are blessed above all mortals. Because you get to work with youth. ●

disciple students

WHEN Josh was in seventh grade I got calls from parents. Other kids' parents. They were frequent and unpleasant, but one stands out in my memory. It came on a Monday morning just before our staff meeting, and my eardrums still hurt. **"*That boy* strangled my daughter with a bicycle tube in *your* Sunday school class and I *demand* to know what you're doing about it!!!"**

"Huh?"

It went downhill from there.

Though Josh never actually injured anyone (that I'm aware of), he did seem capable of it. Between his energy and his arrogance, he came off as unreachable. But we kept trying.

In ninth grade he got cut from basketball. He took it hard and we bore the brunt. So much attitude.

Fast forward to twelfth grade. One week into the school year Josh burst into my office with a freshman guy named Brian. It seems Brian had been cut from the team. For the third time. Three sports in a row—whack, whack, whack. That had to be a record at our school. Most kids sank into depression after one cut. But three?

So there they stood in front of me. Before I could say anything Josh got in my face and announced, "Me and Brian are starting our own basketball league and we need the church gym. You got a problem with that?"

I could hardly speak. It wasn't his attitude that struck me, or even his idea. I love empowering kids and letting them try their ideas. Everybody wins. What struck me was the way Josh was coming alongside Brian. I'd never seen him do that before. Somewhere along the way he'd caught something, and now he was investing energy in someone else. I almost started crying, no joke.

Now, a decade later, Josh has a good job, a wonderful wife, and kids of his own. And this year he's helping oversee the basketball league he and Brian started. You see, their league not only survived—it's become a legend in our area. In its tenth season at this writing, the Blythefield Basketball Association (BBA) is student-led, supports 280 players on 28 teams, and features a website, employees, refs, draft day, trades, a full set of stats, and cell-phone-toting agents. What's more, students share the gospel over one hundred times each year during halftime at these games. As a result, thousands have been introduced to Christ, many join small groups, and sometimes entire families land in church.

There's even a curious twist. The school that cut Brian from three teams now has its state champion football team playing basketball in our league. They've even lost some of their best basketball players to the BBA. And it was Josh's willingness to invest in Brian that made everything happen. Not a bad legacy for an "unreachable" boy.

Sometimes I wish I could redo my phone call with that irate parent because now I know what I'd say. "What do I intend to do about Josh? Keep investing until Christ is formed in him!"

 13 Think long-term

The thrill of working with students is seeing Jesus Christ formed in them. It's one of the biggest adrenaline rushes of life. That's why I was so moved by Josh reaching out to Brian. It signaled Christ gaining ground in his heart.

Guiding students toward spiritual maturity isn't any different from helping them grow in other areas. It takes *regular investments spread over time.* Influence adds up like a stack of newspapers, especially when it's consistent.

The apostle Paul expressed it well:

> *"That's what I'm working so hard at day after day, year after year, doing my best with the energy God so generously gives me"* (Colossians 1:29 MSG).

Don't be discouraged if you've sponsored a powerful event or talked deeply with a student . . . and a week later it seems as if nothing happened. Your influence isn't going to waste. It's adding up. Take the long view and pray for the harvest.

 Describe the future

I nearly got hit by a bus in Chicago because I was gawking at a skyscraper going up next to the river. They were hoisting cauldrons of cement a thousand feet in the air with an enormous crane. Amazing. So here's a question for you. *Do you think architects and engineers were involved?* Or does the construction crew show up every morning and wing it?

In my opinion, the best way to guide students toward spiritual maturity is to develop a tangible description of what a discipled person should look like, then make plans to help students get there before graduation (this is the "Description of a Discipled Person" referenced in #11). So the DDP is part strategy (#11) and part disciple-making action (#14).

I think this is what the apostle Paul was getting at in Colossians 1:28 and Ephesians 4:13 when he spoke of presenting everyone "perfect in Christ," and becoming "mature, attaining to the whole measure of the fullness of Christ." Drafting a compelling DDP will bring clarity and focus to everything you do.

There's no rule that says what a DDP should look like. Think in themes, categories, and characteristics, and try to keep your description to one page. Too much detail and no one will use it. They won't even read it. The action plan can be longer—whatever is necessary to provide guidance and motivate action. But don't create a ball and chain. Also, it should reflect the language your church uses to describe spiritual maturity.

A great way to get started is to gather your team in front of a whiteboard and ask questions. *What does spiritual maturity look like? What character qualities, attitudes, activities, or traits would we expect to see in a fully discipled person? If Jesus were disguised as a student and mingling with our youth, how would we recognize Him?* Push yourselves past the obvious and don't be afraid to thumb through the Gospels as you talk.

To help prime your pump, look at the list that's in the appendix. It's gleaned from what other churches have put on the whiteboard but is in no way exhaustive. Use it as a starting point, and then draw from your own well too. That's the key to ownership.

Once your description is in place, you can use it to make strategic adjustments along the way. For example, let's say one of your descriptions is "Grounded in the Word," but you realize most of your students are biblically illiterate. Because your blueprint has made you aware of the disparity, you can now direct resources toward this area of your plan.

15 Be ready to plant when the ground is fertile

We're all born with a sense that life should work. This is where dreams and expectations come from, and it's especially true of students. The adolescent years can seem like a nonstop rush of selfish demands and pursuits. Speaking at a conference in Philadelphia some years ago, Kevin Huggins observed that young people are always *trying desperately to get something to happen for them* or *keep something from happening to them.* Why? Because life is supposed to work *the way I want it to.*[1]

The thing is, life doesn't work that way, and adolescence is where most people learn that lesson. In fact, not only is life not about us, it often seems against us. Sure, a few kids squeeze through with enough popularity or potential to delay disillusionment for a decade or two, but most will not.

I remember a seventh grader rushing up to me one Sunday morning with flushed cheeks and sparkling eyes. "I have to tell you a secret!" she blurted. "I think Ryan likes me!"

Oh boy. The smile on my face masked the knot in my stomach. Ryan was a gifted young man. Ahead of most sophomores, he was consistently friendly to others, including our junior high students. But what a mismatch.

This poor girl was in the throes of a romantic crush—possibly her first ever. Life was wonderful, and it would work out exactly as she envisioned it.

You and I know better because we've lived more than twelve years. But she certainly did not. Her heart was ripe for a massacre, and that's exactly what happened.

Disillusionment is a shocking reality for students, but it is also a doorway of opportunity God opens for parents and youthworkers to speak to their hearts. Many youth specialists believe that, because adolescent dreams are so pure and sincere, the disillusionment that follows in their wake produces the most fertile "heart soil" to be found in all of life. This is the soil in which you get to plant the seeds of God's love.

16 Remember they're living with upheaval

The transition from childhood to adulthood is one of the prime factors creating opportunity for influence in a young person's life. Students are living through catastrophic upheaval. Child-sized maturity is forced to operate adult-equipped bodies, family trauma, social anxiety, adult expectations, world affairs, daily failures, abuse, the damaging effects of sin, and the growing pains of abstract development. The average adolescent is carrying a stress load that would shut most adults down entirely.

Let's say you approach a middle school student and say, "Tell me about your school." He'll probably respond with, "Well, you go in the main door and turn right to get to my locker." But ask him the same question four years later and you'll hear, "Well, this is supposed to be the best school in our state, but I think it's a joke. The students do such and such and the teachers are always making us do so and so . . ." and on and on. The physiological changes and personal experiences required to move a student from the first answer to the second would take volumes to describe. So if they appear distracted or uninterested, it's not because they don't like you. And it doesn't mean they're not open to your influence. It just means you have to watch for opportunities and bring lots of love with you.

Consider again the words of Paul in Colossians 1:29, this time in a different translation:

"To this end I labor, struggling with all his energy, which so powerfully works in me."

Notice his words: *labor, struggling, energy, powerfully,* and *works.* His language is ripe with the idea of determination and process—neither of which is easy.

Consider a student named Peter who, in seventh grade, decided he was going to make it into the NBA. He had basketball on the brain. Every day he'd shoot five hundred free throws and a thousand lay ups, and every night he'd sleep with the ball. By eighth grade he was hot. The best in his school. Unfortunately, ninth grade was different. Instead of five good players there were two hundred. Though he made the cut, he sat on the bench. Permanently.

The million-dollar observation here is that you have a different Peter in tenth grade than you had in eighth grade. The phrase *God is good* has undergone significant development in his mind. It's no longer a flippant sidebar to his legendary status and popularity (seventh grade). It is now viewed with suspicion and under major attack all the time (tenth grade).

Now, you, the youthworker, step into this situation. Trust develops over time through steady, incremental investments. Scouting games together, shooting hoops in the driveway, and sharing Cokes after school. Though Peter can barely breathe because of his very real pain, a whole new adventure is now underway in his heart. The door to real dialogue has opened (because of his disillusionment), and the conversations that follow will find their way into his prayer life. The topics you address, language you use, questions you ask, and emotions you observe will form the basis of how he understands his story in the context of God's larger story for his life.

It really is your privilege to step into these opportunities. This process is the canvas on which God will repaint the student's definition of *God is good*, so get used to it! You probably know what I'm talking about, because it's probably similar to how God got your attention.

17 Discipleship happens in relationship

In his excellent book *Shaping the Spiritual Life of Students*, Richard Dunn refers to the adult-student relationship as "pacing."

> Pacing requires me to listen to the heart of an adolescent, seeing beyond words and behaviors. Pacing therefore demands time, the time it takes to go beyond the surface in a conversation or to enter the social turf of a student—a band concert, a dorm room. Pacing is costly. The payoff, however, far exceeds the cost. Choosing

to listen or to engage personally an adolescent's world communicates, "Who you are matters to me. I care about what you think, how you feel, and why you make the choices you do." Pacing builds trust. Trust produces relationship. Relationship conceives spiritual life exchanges. Such exchanges are the sacred places where the Holy Spirit reaches through the life of a Christian spiritual caregiver to change forever the life of a student.[2]

Walking together with students is huge. A great transfer takes place within these relationships. Students are enticed to life in Christ through His reality in your life. This bigger adventure gradually overwhelms their more immediate focuses and it supplants their self-centeredness.

How does this happen? Fixing cars, shopping together, playing cards, or watching one of their games is the stuff in your toolbox. Early on, younger students will leave messages on your phone that reek with self-centered, undecipherable chatter. Most of the time they'll even forget to mention their name or number. Six years later those same students will leave stunning messages filled with passion and concern. Your responsibility as a youthworker is not to change every student overnight. Rather, it is to walk alongside them during their "fertile heart" years.

You can't "pace" with thirty kids from the front of a classroom. Nor can one person single-handedly "pace" with thirty kids outside of a classroom. That's why we use lots of volunteer help with our group, and we try to find adults who are willing to stick with the same two or three students for the duration of their time in high school. Here are a few examples of how "pacing" might look over the years:

- **Face-to-face**—This involves a sit-down talk at a place like Starbucks, McDonald's, or Dairy Queen.

- **Shoulder to shoulder**—These conversations happen while walking or driving someplace. They can be direct one-to-one appointments or talks that occur in the middle of an event or trip.

- **Task-centered talk**—If the above options seem too direct, I'll often use a task as an excuse. Fixing cars together, hiring students for yard work, shopping for supplies, running errands, or attending a sporting event all make use of some outside factor to reduce the direct nature of talking.

Most adults feel too busy for this type of investment, so how can we keep pace with students on top of everything else we're involved in? Here are a few ways to slice and dice it:

- **Recognition**—Building relationships with students requires many small investments. Call out to them as you pass in the hall, and try to use their names. It's surprising what two-minute conversations in the hallway at church can yield, particularly when you comment on something meaningful to them.

- **Intersections**—Most of us shop for groceries, get haircuts, eat out, and hire babysitters. Be intentional with these tasks and use them to cross paths with students who work in such places or need pocket money.

- **Shared circles**—The biggest opportunities for influence happen in circles that naturally coincide. Which students do you often see? They might be neighbors, children of friends, members of your small group, or even friends of your own kids. Because you live in shared circles you have heightened access to their lives. Take the time to learn who they are, what they are involved in, and how their walk with Christ is going. These will likely be the ones who, in twenty years, will still remember your involvement in their lives.

- **Crisis**—Students are often involved in crisis situations, some real and some imagined. It's good to be available in such situations, though it's also good to have a referral list in your pocket. If you're a volunteer, keep a few phone numbers handy (parents, youthworkers, and so on). I have a series of counselors I refer students and parents to even though I've been counseling students for decades. This takes the pressure off in terms of legal liabilities and technical responses, yet allows me to do what I do best—being there for them. In the end it's the consistent friendship and support that remains meaningful to them.

18 Pain = opportunity

Pan can be overwhelming. In *The Problem of Pain,* C. S. Lewis observes that God uses pain as a megaphone to get people's attention. Even so, we know from Scripture that the fundamental problem of life is not pain. Pain is a consequence of a much larger issue —an issue Christ addressed with decisiveness and finality at the cross. Being separated from God because of sin is the source of our mess. Never forget this. It will keep you on track as you face a steady stream of broken lives.

To acknowledge a student's pain, to cry with her, and to care about her is to be like Christ. But a great risk plays out at this level. If we reinforce her notion that "pain is my biggest problem," we do her an injustice. Such thinking makes it more difficult for Christ to be formed in her. For the truth is that no matter what a student has been through, her experience has landed on a fully developed grid of stubborn, self-centered assumptions. You'll never be able to provide lasting help unless you—at some point—lead her into an awareness of her true problem. She is a sinner by birth, choice, and practice. All of us are. Period.

All the same, pain still offers an effective opportunity to lead students deeper in their faith. At some point the pain they experience will cause them to ask deep questions. *Can God be trusted? Did He cause what I'm experiencing? How can a good God seem so uncaring?* Such questions must be asked for this process of faith to be deepened.

When it comes to discussing pain with students, it's helpful to explore the peaks and valleys of their lives. You might try having them draw a line on a piece of paper representing their lives to this point. An upward bend signifies a positive memory while a downward turn means the opposite. As they talk, they may share three or four such events. Listen carefully, and always pray for wisdom to hear the right things.

Here are two main things to listen for:

- **Emotion**—Emotions reveal the price tags of events and relationships.[3] When you see their eyes mist up, make a mental note of it.

- **Deflection**—Students are like us. When the data becomes too hot, they deflect through humor or random subject changing. Pay attention when this happens.

I remember connecting with one of our students on a trip. Though attractive and seemingly personable, her defensive style of relating kept everyone at arm's length. I was puzzled by this until, nearly a week into it, she revealed a dark and horrific story. Abuse had shattered her adolescence and imprisoned her heart. The following sentences defined her perception of life:

- *I can never undo the past.*
- *I can't shake the memories.*
- *The betrayal is overwhelming.*
- *My life is ruined.*
- *I must protect myself.*
- *I must keep a safe distance between myself and others.*

Notice her preoccupation with self and pain. Admittedly, it makes sense—she was reeling from severe trauma. The thing is, there's no salvation or healing in self-protection. It actually makes matters worse. In her case, her self-protective, mysterious style of relating drove guys crazy. They either stayed away or pursued her for the wrong reasons. Both results exaggerated her need to be loved and reinforced her decision to protect herself.

The explosive joy of working with students is to offer them hope as found in relationship with Jesus Christ. Awaken their hope and shift their focus from unsolvable problems to a problem that actually has a solution! But don't misunderstand me as saying this is an easy process. It requires much prayer, time, trust, and study (remember Paul's words in Colossians 1:29). Yet redemption does lie down that path.

19 Learn the art of real conversation

Two things happen as you grow in relationship with students. First, they catch the direction of your life. You become a visual aid to supplement the Christian theory they hear at church. Second, they understand God better as you mimic His love. None of this happens at once. It takes many interactions—each flavored with conversation that says you care about them. Here are a few insights I've found to be helpful when it comes to talking with students:

- **Build an emotional vocabulary**—If disillusionment provides a doorway into the heart, words supply the key to open it. Students have strong emotional swings but often lack the ability to articulate what they feel like. Our job is to help them put words to feelings. After a student has revealed a particularly difficult situation, I'll often say something like, "Can you think of a stronger word to describe what you're going through?" I give them permission to fully express the brokenness of life. Only by facing reality (the problem of sin) do they move toward maturity.

- **Advance and retreat**—It's easy to tell when your questions invade "sacred" places. Students get uneasy and demonstrate plenty of nonverbal communication. Pay close attention to this and balance the heat. Probe and back off. After a while, they know that you know what's going on, and it eases their ability to talk about it. It could take a week or a month. Maybe a year. But we're in this for the long haul anyway.

- **Don't fix it**—The statement *God is good* won't fix a student's life, nor does it help to try and fix his problems in the space of a thirty-minute conversation. *God is good* is a lifetime adventure that becomes central as we: (1) experience the brokenness of life, and (2) surrender our shriveled stories to God in favor of His Grand Adventure.

- **Don't be fooled by apathy**—A common problem we face with today's students is apathy. There is a general attitude of shoulder shrugging or dispassionate, cryptic responses. Even though this feels bad, don't be put off by it. Try to remember that people are created to be passionate. Therefore, apathy is a chosen behavior, a feeble attempt at self-protection. If you persist you'll discover what stirs them, and then you can enter that place. Always partner with God through prayer. Pray as you talk with students. Probe various areas of their lives. Gradually, you'll note softenings or openings as students begin to feel loved. Remember—*you don't have the ability to change them*, so the pressure's off. Just loving them where they're at is the best antidote to apathy.

- **Remain calm with self-hatred**—It's easy to overreact when faced with symptoms of self-hatred (e.g., eating disorders, cutting, substance abuse, and so on). In reality, this is part of the sin cycle for every human being. However, when students act it out in the harsh manner of adolescence, we get hyper. Check yourself by asking and reflecting on what is underneath their surface behavior. All behavior is purposeful, so the real question is *why*. Don't hesitate to take precautionary measures if you believe their safety and/or immediate health is at stake. Otherwise, keep moving into their lives, even when their behavior says, "you're not welcome here."

Ask the right questions

Our culture isn't very good at dialogue. Mostly we get monologue or random talking. So it's important to use questions effectively. Having the ability to ask the right questions will help you know, care for, and equip your students. What you're after is a meaningful exchange of thoughts and ideas—and believe me, you'll both enjoy it. Here are several techniques that work well with our group:

- **Open-ended questions**—Questions that begin with *what, why,* and *how* are likely to invite thoughtful discussion. On the other hand, questions that can be answered with one word cause conversation to shrivel. Why? Because I'm insulting a student's intelligence if I reduce her to shrugs and yes-or-no answers. Have you ever been frustrated by a "this is going nowhere" conversation with a student? Most likely the problem was *did you, are you,* or *can you* questions. In retrospect, "Are you a freshman?" is perhaps the stupidest question I've ever asked. Try it some time. Watch the student shrink to the back of his chair. Nah, don't even try it. Instead, come up with questions that invite thoughtful interaction and watch that same student come alive.

- **"I'm listening" questions**—It's great to listen. It's even better to demonstrate by asking follow-up questions and making restatements. For example, "Well, let me ask you this then . . ." or "If I'm hearing you right you're saying . . ." Work hard on your listening skills. The fact that you care to listen sends a powerful message. Conversely, so does not listening. If you customarily interrupt or co-opt ("Hey, that reminds me of a time when I . . ."), they quickly get the message.

- **Springboard questions**—There are certain questions that almost always move students deeper. A few I use regularly include:

  FACTS: What happened?

  FEELINGS: What was that like for you? What'd you think about it?

  RESPONSE: What did you do? How did you respond? How'd that work out for you?

  MOTIVE: Why do you think you responded that way?

- **The trick of the third person**—When a conversation seems slow, too direct, or just plain difficult, it's helpful to bring another "person" into it. For example, students love talking about what others think. Instead of, "What do you think about the new coach?" you might try, "What does your friend Beth think about your new coach?" You're not really talking about Beth—she's just serving as the narrator to help your student express her thoughts.

- **Key players**—Asking questions about their most significant relationships is crucial. For instance, "Who do you talk with more, your mom or dad?" is a great lead-in question which often invites the student to explain why. Or another good one is: "How deep do conversations usually go with your dad compared to when you speak with your best friend?" Such questions will help you assess how connected a student is at home.

21 Enlist an army of praying people

Elsewhere I've referenced Ben Patterson's remark that prayer is the work and ministry is the fruit. Let's take that one step further. Let's say it applies to everything you do with students. You faithfully serve them and God brings the fruit. Don't underestimate God's role in the spiritual growth of your students. As R. A. Torrey writes in *How to Pray*:

> We live in a day characterized by the multiplication of man's machinery and the diminution of God's power. The great cry of our day is work, work, work, new organizations, new methods, new machinery; the great need of our day is prayer.[5]

One way to pull this off is to enlist the people of your church to pray for your students—*specifically by name*. A good way to make this happen is to delegate the organization of it to students (expose them to prayer and all ventures related to prayer). Find several who do photography, administration, and graphic design, and have them catalog all the students in your group. Gather everyone's picture, name, school year, and whatever else you think would be helpful (digital cameras and computers make this easy). Then have them print out a small flyer or "baseball card" on each student.

Your job is to decide who the praying people are at your church. Maybe it's the elders and deacons. Or the women's Bible study. Or all the parents. Or the retired people. Figure out who does the heavy lifting when it comes to prayer and make sure they get those cards. If you have more cards than praying people, give everybody a few. Even better, if you have more praying people, make duplicate cards so all your students are prayed for by multiple people.

You can decide how much of this to delegate to students rather than doing it yourself, but the key is to generate prayer for those kids and see God work on their behalf.

What if you don't know who does the praying at your church? Sometimes it's hard to tell. Then your adventure for the month is discovering who it is. Ask around—people love giving opinions about such things. Eventually you'll learn who's who.

I also have people pray for issues and events as well as students. (The more prayer the better. That's why Sonlife Ministries has "Developing a prayer base" as one of its six pillars.) My practice is to engage beginners with general requests to get them on the team and set them afire. (Fan those flames whenever possible.) The more diligence a person shows, the weightier the challenges I ask them to tackle. And it's important to have a few veterans you can turn to with confidential matters and spiritual warfare issues.

Oh, that I would pray as fervently as some of our people. But thank God for putting them here to work on behalf of our youth.

22 Teach them what the Bible says

We know the irreplaceable role Scripture plays in our own discipleship. It's as important as food. Yet a tension comes into play as we "pace" with students. Is faith taught or caught? How about maturity? How can a student receive God's Word if he doesn't have any context for why it matters?

I've seen conversations go from fire to ice in ten seconds once I start talking about the Bible. Yet, I've also seen the living Word bring life to dead souls. There are no formulas or systems that eliminate this tension. However, a couple of principles can be gleaned from how Jesus discipled those closest to Him:

- **Responsibility**—Help students take responsibility for their own faith. Forcing a student through catechism can turn indifference to defiance (unless you have a world-class teacher). But challenging a student to grow strong spiritually, or to learn what the Bible says about some hot topic will allow his enthusiasm to gain momentum. Creating an appetite beats force-feeding every time. Especially when the student has observed your authentic hunger for the Word.

- **The Word, unplugged**—There's a passage in Luke 4 where Jesus reads a portion of Scripture to the people and tells them it's about Him. That's it! You don't always need a lesson. Just read them something and tell them what it means.

- **All you can eat**—Jesus fed His listeners according to their appetites. From stories for the masses to detailed instructions for the devoted. Serve up what your students can take, but make sure none go home hungry.

- **Love before lessons**—Relational investment opens the door for content. Once a student is convinced you're there for her, she will read and consider the Scriptures you pass her way.

- **Incentives**—This is always heavily debated. Some churches give kids candy if they'll memorize verses. Other churches condemn such tricks. The truth is that Jesus' teachings often included incentive and reward. I think it's okay to use incentives in a limited way to help students bring God's Word into their lives. We sometimes offer financial assistance for trips to those students who engage in specific reading, memorizing, or Bible study assignments.

- **Resources**—Jesus used a variety of teaching techniques to help His followers remember truth. He used props, current events, hands-on experiences, and so on. Today there are hundreds of options at our fingertips. Books, discussion guides, MP3s, DVDs, journals, packaged activities, field trips, and on and on. Students vary in terms of aptitude and learning style, so utilize a variety of resources to help them learn.

23 Attempt great things (even if you might fail)

I won't quote it here because I've already seen it in too many books, but Teddy Roosevelt's quote about attempting bold things is a bull's-eye. Don't hesitate to attempt great things, even though you will sometimes fail. Flexibility (in failure) has got to become a youthworker's middle name.

Several years ago we field-tested a discipleship strategy that called for enrolling an additional one hundred adults into an already busy program. Even today I am convinced it would have made an incalculable difference in the spiritual lives of our students. In fact, I considered it revolutionary. But we couldn't pull it off. Most adults are stretched so thin between church, work, and family, they just can't sustain any more commitments.

I understand this and accept it (especially here in Michigan where, at the time of this writing, things are tight economically). So we shelved our plans, learned some things, and continued to look for other ways to meet our students' spiritual needs.

But I'm still glad we tried, because trial and error is good fertilizer for improvement, and that's my goal. ●

cultivate groups

A few weeks ago my wife and I were in the family room surrounded by students. Four were crammed on the couch, one filled the love seat—horizontally—and several were sprawled on the floor.

Then it happened. Heather started talking about her childhood.

She remembered being eight years old and sitting downstairs in the rec room with Missy, her cat, asleep on her lap. Missy was old and Heather's parents often talked of putting her to sleep . . . forever.

Heather could hear loud voices upstairs, and they sounded scary. As the shouting grew more angry, she began to cry, linking the yelling with her fear of losing Missy. That's when the door opened.

"Heather," called her father, "will you come upstairs please?"

The knot in her stomach tightened. What would they say? She placed Missy on the couch and gently propped pillows around her so she'd be safe. Then, with great dread, she climbed the stairs.

Rounding the corner from the kitchen into the living room she was surprised to see her older sister there. Mom, Dad, and Stephanie, all looking down. And not smiling.

She sat on the loveseat, close to Stephanie, and noticed that she didn't make a face at her. She didn't even look at her. In fact, no one would look at her, and she knew why. They're going to take Missy away . . .

Unable to hold it in, she blurted, "I promise to take better care of her! She's just tired right now, but she'll get better—please don't put her to sleep!" With tears streaming down her cheeks she pleaded with them to spare Missy's life.

And then she stopped, mid-sentence. Her mom was staring at her with a confused look on her face. She didn't seem angry, but sad. In fact, she was crying! Heather had never seen her mom cry before. Ever. The pain in her stomach grew worse and she could hardly breath.

Finally, after several failed attempts, her mother managed a few awkward words, "Your father and I have decided it would be best if I moved out of the house for a while." She opened her mouth like she wanted to say more, then shook her head, got up, and left the room. They heard the side door close and the family was broken. Forever.

Wow. We all sat there staring at Heather, holding our breath. Even the guys were transfixed. For the first time they saw past her looks and into her eyes—glazed with tears, haunted by pain.

Most of our group knew Heather's parents were divorced. She'd told us months ago. A perfunctory comment. A piece of data passed along. But this night we were invited into the life of a vulnerable child; a little girl whose greatest fear had previously been losing a pet.

When the young grow old in a moment's time, their protected world shattered by pain, they never forget. And when one of them transports you back to that flashpoint, community is forged on the spot. By fire.

---

24 Feed their hunger for relationships

Today's students are ravished by culture and starved for relationship. The speed of living has bypassed the support systems of adolescence, leaving them exposed and vulnerable. The story of their lives unfolds without the benefit of life-related mentoring, and the customs and responsibilities that once transported children to adulthood have been replaced by a nonstop parade of demands and activities.

It's the frenetic life.

Imagine a girl named Gina who hasn't had a real conversation with her parents in over a year. Consequently, some of her questionable relationships with peers have become more invasive and influential than ever. As her attitude and relational style head south, so do her relationships at home. She knows instinctively things are not going well, but doesn't really know why. Nor does she have time to worry about it between the competing demands of school, work, friends, sports, media, guys, coaches, and so on.

Now imagine inserting another obligation into her frenzy. One of her friends invites her to a small group, and since busyness is practically worshipped nowadays, she adds it to her insane schedule. What happens next? Two things. *First*, she is pursued by people who actually listen to her. Who hear the meaning behind her words and seem interested in the person within the package.

At some point tears begin to flow. Uneasy, she fights them back, but the way these people talk with her, it's as if they really care. Something inside comes alive—something so deep she'd forgotten it was there.

Then the *second* thing happens. She experiences God's presence during group prayer. Between prayers comes a silence. A quietness foreign to Gina, who can't survive twenty seconds without her iPod blaring and her cell phone ringing.

God is taking hold of her heart, thawing that which has been frozen a long time. He is feeding a starved soul.

Groups provide a purposeful opportunity to let relationally hungry students feast on God's goodness. And, since they're as flexible as water, you don't need more money, space, or time to get started. Your only challenge will be growing leaders fast enough, and we'll address that in chapter 10.

25 Healthy groups share lives

To insist groups must follow a prescribed order is like telling the wind when to blow. Group gatherings don't unfold in equal segments—but they *do* function better when certain elements are included. Our leaders rely on four essentials to keep their groups healthy. No two groups practice them the same way, but you'll find all four in every healthy group we sponsor:

- *Life-sharing*
- *Prayer*
- *Truth*
- *Outflow*

Life-sharing is what brings meaning to a group. It's the relational context from which all the rest of it flows. Some time ago, the late H. Stephen Glenn[5] brought the term *dialogue* into popular usage by noting its absence from family life. A paraphrase of his definition reveals its centrality within a group setting:

Dialogue is the meaningful exchange of perceptions and values within a group of people who vary in experience and intellectual-spiritual development.

The word *meaningful* is a joke when it comes to most family interaction. "Pass the ketchup" or "Make sure you're home by midnight" don't even make first cuts. Current studies on family discussions are alarming. For most families, when you eliminate nonimportant banter, there is zero dialogue happening.

The word *perceptions* is also insightful. Since behavior is more often based on perception than truth, we expose the control center of how people operate when we explore their perceptions.

Finally, the terms *experience* and *development* are worth noting. Throw a group of peers together and nothing too significant happens. Why? Because their experience base and level of development are relatively uniform.

Teenagers actually prefer hanging out with older people. Do you believe that statement? Many don't at first glance, but it's true. In fact, it's rooted in basic human need. Survival requires learning, whereas the definition of a peer is "one who knows no more about life than I do."

Life-sharing transports us back to the time when pivotal events formed and shaped us, and it can happen in your group whether you're working with five, seven, or even ten students (six or seven is ideal). When Heather brought us back to the point of her family's breakdown, our entire group dynamic changed. In one evening we learned how to care. And be cared for.

26 Healthy groups teach truth

"I tried the Bible but it doesn't relate to my life."

Kids love this line and use it all the time. You'll hear it again and again. And the best response is, "Exactly!" They have the right idea, just backwards. Students who utter such complaints see themselves as the center of the universe and they see the Bible as a dust-gathering relic. But their reasoning is flipped around. They're the dust and the Word is eternal. When kids get stuck in *now* they lose perspective on *forever*. And *forever* is what really matters.

Don't ever surrender the fact that the Bible is every student's essential reference point. Happiness, relationships, pain, courage, anxiety, love, fear, maturity, possessions, hope, sexuality, forgiveness, the spiritual realm, and a million other things all find their source in the Bible. It's the most relevant thing in life and it comes to them at a point when their worldview is being forged. The timing couldn't be better.

Helping students take responsibility for their spiritual development is crucial, and it won't happen without the Bible. Though you'll face an uphill battle with some (perhaps many), I've found the following strategies helpful:

- **Supplement** —Trendy stuff may seem more relevant than the Bible, but it's not. There will always be another book, and last year's new book will seem stale compared to next year's book. Not that I have anything against books (you're reading one right now and I hope it's helpful). Just don't use books or any other stuff as the main attraction. Use it to supplement your study of the Bible. Use it to provide enhancement or application, not illumination.

- **Think time**—The more time you allow yourself, the more power your insights will have. We've all had plenty of practice at "winging it," you know, preparing fifteen minutes before teaching a lesson. The influence those lessons wield is generally sub-par, right? So don't approach the task of preparation as one big assignment. Break it down. Take five minutes at the beginning of the week to determine a topic. Once the topic is lodged in your mind, you'll see other points, stories, and experiences filtered by that topic. Applications will follow, your teaching of God's Word will gain color, and your lessons will gain traction in the lives of your students.

- **Bible options**—There's more than one way to expose students to the Bible. You can read it out loud whenever you're together. One youthworker I know has a pocket edition he takes everywhere. His students have heard the Word in the woods, on mountains, rivers, and beaches, under the stars, at restaurants—anywhere the moment is right and his pocket edition is handy. Another group sponsors Scripture memory, sometimes motivating students with special events or celebrations when they've all mastered a passage. Some promote reading through the Bible every year and distribute Bible reading charts every January with regular accountability. We create study booklets using Bible passages to teach on topics relevant to our own group. The options are myriad, and there is no formula. But one thing is certain—it only takes one student to catch the vision and the momentum soon works its way through the entire group.

27 Healthy groups pray purposefully

Every kid needs a campfire. A place to circle the wagons, find safety, and gain rest. Prayer provides this. It connects my story with God's story, bringing our daily lives together. For the young, prayer almost always errs on the side of "my" story. But that's normal, and life is all about moving in God's direction. A worthy goal to keep in mind for your groups is that every student grow in his or her ability to pray.

Most students come to us without categories of prayer, so we start them off with the popular ACTS acrostic—Adoration, Confession, Thanksgiving, and Supplication—as follows:

- **Adoration**—Talk to God about what He's like or what you've read about Him. Tell Him about the things you've seen Him do. Get creative and consider the things around you, the human body, laws of nature, or whatever is part of His work.

This category helps students see beyond themselves, opens their eyes to the greater character of God, and challenges them to stretch—to give a name to His various characteristics. It further helps students gain perspective about their rightful place.

- **Confession**—In what ways does your life not measure up to the example of Christ and the standard of God's holiness? How about your group? Is there anything you need to collectively confess before God? Be as discreet as you need to be, but also be honest.

Confession of sin as a small group is a deep and profound way to connect with the grace of God. It realigns peer-positioning. God is God and we are not. We're all at the same "in need of forgiveness" level. Dietrich Bonhoeffer remarks on this in his book *Life Together*:

> We do not complain of what God does not give us; we rather thank God for what He does give us daily. And is not what has been given us enough: brothers, who will go on living with us through sin and need under the blessing of His grace? Even when sin and misunderstanding burden the communal life, is not the sinning brother still a brother, with whom I, too, stand under the Word of Christ? Will not his sin be a constant occasion for me to give thanks that both of us may live in the forgiving love of God in Jesus Christ?[6]

Any type of community that builds itself on a dream of warm fuzzies is a joke. The truth is we're a mess, and we must begin to be disillusioned by ourselves and each other before we can truly experience the grace and forgiveness of Christ. It is the repetition of this need and supply that truly forms community.

- **Thanksgiving**—Start with whatever comes to mind first. What do you have that others don't? What blessings are you aware of or what afflictions have you not had to bear? What can you see that's good in the other members of your group? Thanksgiving is like a snowball rolling downhill.

- **Supplication**—Needs and requests related to you or others. Physical, spiritual, emotional—group or personal.

Most students excel at this. Recognizing needs of heart, body, and relationship comes naturally because we're needy people.

Make sure to have supplication follow the other forms of prayer so it is contained in balance. When I truly adore Christ and confess who I am before Him, and when I offer prayers of thanksgiving for who He is and what He has done, my own needs are even clearer. They are also contained in a more humble place.

There's nothing magical about the ACTS model of prayer. It's simply a useful tool—easy to remember and simple to follow—to help groups of students grow their relationship with God, and with each other in the process.

28 Healthy groups give generously

What would you rather do? Jump into a stagnant, slime-covered pond, or dive into a crystal clear pool surrounded by large boulders and fed by a mountain stream?

With that answer in mind, who would you rather spend time with? Someone trapped by her own self-interests, or a person who gives freely from the depth of her character?

Groups are the same way. They can be full of life, or stagnant and self-focused. One way to keep things healthy is to regularly give to others. Every group has something to give—time, resources, energy, and so forth. The key is to realize this and build it into your group schedule.

Last night, one of our small groups got together and cooked several meals for a needy family. They spent the entire night cooking, laughing, wrapping, and freezing food. No prayer, and no Bible study. They simply gave. And everyone left the group glowing.

29 Learn how to listen and then actually listen . . .

The next time you're with a group of students, monitor their conversation. It will most likely be dominated by co-opting or interrupting, as follows:

- **Co-opting** occurs when I tolerate your words just long enough to identify a superior story of my own. The split second you take a breath, I take over.

- **Interrupting** is even more blatant. It says, "Your thoughts and experience are of no consequence and mine are so much more profound I needn't even wait for you to take a breath before butting in."

If you intend to lead students into dialogue, you'll need to teach them how to listen. Most students have never thought about how they communicate, and actually respond well to simple, grace-based coaching. And it sure makes a difference in a group setting. To teach them how to honor one another with careful listening, consider these simple tools:

- **Restatements** reveal my interest as I seek to understand what you mean: "If I'm hearing you right, you're nervous about this upcoming family gathering. Is that correct?"

- **Follow-up questions** build on my interest by demonstrating that I care about what is happening with you: "If what you're saying turns out to be true, how will you handle it?"

We touched on these conversation tools in chapter 3. In that context (discipleship) they related to how we pursue students. Here they have to do with how students relate to each other. In our mostly self-centered universe it makes all the difference in the world if these small groups of students have the ability to actually listen and speak truth into each other's lives. A little honor and courtesy goes a long way in bonding a group together.

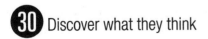 **30** Discover what they think

Ever notice how many interviewers discredit their guests? Suppose you flip on the news just in time to hear about new tensions in the

Middle East. The host, warming to the sound of his own voice, turns to an esteemed guest and says:

"With over forty years of experience in this region, Dr. Smith is our nation's foremost expert on tensions in the Middle East. Thank you, Dr. Smith, for joining us this morning to help us understand what might be at the root of this current crisis. I, for one, would like to know what we should expect regarding this week's escalation in violence. I mean, from my point of view, it seems we've been here before in both Korea and Vietnam, and you would think our leaders would have learned a few lessons from those engagements. But that doesn't seem to be the case. I mean, just think about what happens every time the military takes such extreme measures with apparent disregard for a civilian population. Did you see yesterday's footage of the situation?"

First of all, notice how the nonexpert essentially steals the stage from the expert. Then consider how his question limits the expert to a *yes* or *no* answer. Honestly, if his objective was to interview himself, why bother inviting a guest?

Consider what help and enlightenment the expert might have offered if the question had been phrased differently.

Dr. Smith, from your experience, how do you see these tensions playing out over the next twelve months?

Now we can learn something!

Asking good questions means knowing how to frame them and caring what others think. Again, noted author and conference speaker Stephen Glenn is humorous as he exposes the shallow tendencies of most conversations. Questions that begin with *did you, can you, can't you, will you, won't you,* and *aren't you* require no more than a shrug or a grunt in response. They're an affront to one's intelligence.

You and your leaders will do better with open-ended questions like these:

- *What is your opinion . . . ?*

- *How would you describe . . . ?*

- *Why is it that . . . ?*

One of the great gifts we can give students is the ability to grow their dialogue skills. By modeling careful listening and thoughtful questioning in our groups, we can equip them to engage in meaningful, life-changing conversations. And as these conversations begin to actually take place, they will begin to help the group dynamic along by prodding students toward their individual areas of concern.

31 It's good when leaders lead differently

A year ago, two group leaders approached me within the same week. The first asked, "Is it permissible to take our group to a musical that one of our students is in? If so, how should we handle transportation?" The second said, "Our group is talking about a trip to Guatemala to work at an orphanage. You good with that?"

Group leaders come in all shapes and styles. Some are wild mavericks while others thrive on specific guidance. The diversity is remarkable, and I believe such differences strengthen our team. The maverick can learn responsibility from the leader who is systematic and thoughtful, while the cautious leader can learn vision and faith from the risk-taking pioneer. So honor the strengths of each style and help them see value in other's gifts. Your students will be blessed as a result.

 Find time to train your leaders

Most of us are out-of-control busy. That means there is no perfect time for training. Meeting every Saturday morning for ten weeks doesn't work anymore. Yet that doesn't mean we can dispense with training (unless you enjoy endless headaches and massive turnover). It simply means coming up with creative and flexible ways to train and support. Here are a few suggestions that have worked well for us:

ELECTIVES:
- Offer regular training modules that are short and helpful
- Make some introductory and others advanced
- Offer them more than once and at flexible times
- Make them available when people are already at the church (like during Sunday school)

MODELING:
- Visit a small group that one of your leaders is overseeing
- Give them a break by running the group that night
- Model teaching, leading discussion, and prayer

CONSULTING:
- Ask group leaders if they need help with any of their kids
- Take that student out for a one-on-one checkup
- Report back to the group leader with insights and prayer opportunities
- Seek out someone who will pray for the students in every group

RESOURCES:
- Stay up to date with available material
- Always feed Podcasts, books, and articles to your leaders
- Bring some of your leaders to youthworker conferences every year

- Handle the busy work for them by building their email lists and contact information

33 Define each group's purpose

When my daughter was seventeen, she ran a group of junior high students (and lived to tell about it!). A month into her group experience one of her students asked if she could invite a friend. This is a good thing, right? Imagine the look on my daughter's face when this kid walked in with four new girls the following week. The entire climate of the group changed in an instant.

It's important for group leaders to decide at the beginning of each group season whether they want "open" or "closed" groups.

Open groups are committed to outreach. Their goal is to attract new students and expose them to faith in Christ. Open groups regularly expand, divide, and multiply.

Closed groups are different. They thrive on continuity, which is necessary for the pursuit of spiritual formation through depth of sharing and commitment. Adding new people to a closed group presents the near impossible challenge of bringing them up to speed.

34 Think: growth by groups

Groups are an explosive way to grow a youth ministry. Significant teenaged (and all-aged) social favor rests on the idea of joining a group. I ask kids all the time if they want to join a small group—apathetic kids, arrogant kids, needy kids, aloof kids—and the response is nearly always the same. *Sure!*

Years ago, when I had all the answers to life, I was very protective of our groups. I limited their number and never put friends in the same group. (Hey, they should meet new people, right?) Then I was challenged by a guy who had about eight million groups going at his church. He asked me a simple question, "Who is better equipped to reach new students than their friends?" Can't argue with that. So now we challenge all our "open group" students to pray for three friends. And guess what? Pretty soon the group is too big (more than twelve students, for instance), the leader must divide the group in half, and they are scrambling to find a new leader. What a great problem to have! (More on this in a minute.)

Let's say there are eighteen students at your church. Half want to form a closed group, while the others prefer an open group. If the kids in your open group faithfully pray for three friends each, you'll have at least two open groups by the end of the school year, and maybe another closed group. Two years down the road you might have three and seven, and so on. Plus, at least some of these kids' parents will be visiting your church to see what is going on.

The point is, when you launch groups, be thinking growth. And make sure the church is thinking about what to do with new families, because they may just show up . . .

35 Always pick an apprentice

Since most of our groups are run by volunteers, there are many times when a leader can't make a meeting. Business trips, vacations, weddings, other meetings at work or church—few volunteers can swing an entire year of perfect attendance. Plus, some groups multiply several times each year, which means new leaders for every offshoot. That's why I tell our leaders to begin each new season with an apprentice in mind. Some use students and others prefer adults. Both are good, and a thriving group program typically requires both.

I always use the first few months of our group season to delegate all the facets of running a group to my apprentice. Sometimes I'll have him arrange snacks while other times he'll prepare lessons.

Once in a while I'll even have him take a student out for a one-on-one session. Be proactive. It's simply a matter of time before you'll need another leader, and hands-on experience provides the best training.

36 Treat problems as access points

Working with people is messy. Jesus Himself observed: "It is not those who are well who need a physician, but those who are sick" (Luke 5:31 NASB). Problems will always spring up because of the brokenness of life. Don't panic.

Problems are good because they reveal opportunities. They're like growing pains. Here are various examples I'm sure you'll face:

- Students wanting to switch groups

- Leaders wanting to quit

- Everyone talking, nobody listening

- Houses getting trashed

- Student leaders who are proud

- Students wanting to be in the same group as their new boyfriend/girlfriend

- Oops, now they want to be in another group because they just got dumped

- Poor leadership

- Students driving other students without parental permission (or knowledge . . .)

- Kids showing up early/late and leaving late/early

- Inappropriate relationships

- Rebellion and corrosive attitudes

- Heresy or spiritual experiences your church doesn't approve of

- Fights, arguments, and general ugliness

Will these experiences be difficult? You bet. Are they bad? That depends on why you're working with youth. If it's to provide a better alternative to the social scene at school, problems will be the bane of your experience. But if you see them as access points for the redemptive power of Jesus Christ in the lives of your students (and leaders!), your experience will be deep, stretching, and rich.

The bottom line is that your leaders will need help. When trials come, only those who are supported will stick around for more than one season. That's why problem solving must be a priority for the overseer. This translates into ongoing involvement, coaching, and prayer. And it reveals a God who uses the drama of daily life to bless His children. As James wrote, "Consider it a sheer gift, friends, when tests and challenges come at you from all sides. . . . Let it do its work so you become mature and well-developed, not deficient in any way" (from James 1:2, 4 MSG). ●

prioritize

WE were only fifteen minutes into our first date in weeks when the doorbell rang. It was 9:30 p.m., very dark outside, and I had an immediate internal reaction. Who dares invade my personal life?

You have to understand something. For two exhausted adults with three little kids and the endless demands of a youth ministry schedule, a hot date meant catching an hour before bed to sit on the couch and compare schedules. We hadn't spent meaningful time together in forever.

And now someone was at the door.

I considered ignoring it, but my conscience protested. Besides, whoever it was kept ringing the bell. With a burdened sigh I rose from the couch.

There at the door stood a student grinning ear to ear. I hadn't seen him in three years. Not that I hadn't tried. After dozens of unreturned calls and messages, I'd reluctantly moved on to other kids. Now he was on my front porch and my heart was sinking fast.

"Hey Don! Guess what I'm doing!"

"What are you doing?" I asked, searching my soul for some shred of other-centeredness.

"I'm leaving for the army at six o'clock in the morning!"

He grinned. I stared.

"So, anyway, I just thought I'd come over and talk for a while since I'm kinda nervous about the whole thing."

My heart landed with a thud.

Rather than invite him in I stepped outside in my socks. And there I stood, freezing cold and frantically searching for some remedy. Should I hang out with him for a couple of hours and mend fences with Julie later? Or should I blow off his apparent need and honor my wife?

What would you do?

37 Make personal priorities . . . and live by them

Whether you're a parent, volunteer, intern, or full-time youthworker, working with students often means making choices between good and good. That's why you *must* set priorities. It's the only way to achieve congruence between what you believe and how you invest your time.

Let's go back to the front porch. As I stood there shivering, a thought came to me. "Hey Lee," I said. "Thanks for coming over and letting me in on your life. What time did you say you're leaving tomorrow?"

He replied as before, "Six o'clock."

"Good," I said. "That will give us plenty of time in the morning. You see, I'm in the middle of something I can't reschedule, but I'd love to hear your plans. How about meeting me at Denny's at 3:00 a.m.?"

I'll never forget the look on his face. *Are you insane? There's no way I'm getting up that early!* What he managed to say was, "Um, I'm not sure I can make it at three. Would five o'clock be okay with you?"

Right then it was clear. His need was neither life threatening nor critical. Otherwise he would have met me early.

Some might judge me as uncaring. Others might think I did the right thing. Either way, don't miss the tension. There will always be tension when choosing between good and good. To live well without tension is impossible. *To decide well without priorities is also impossible.*

Five years earlier, when I transitioned from volunteering to working full-time with our youth, I carefully developed a list of priorities. Though basic, it addressed all the key areas of my life:

1. Love God first and most

2. Love my wife as Christ loves the Church

3. Love my children and give them a taste of God's goodness

4. Work hard *and* smart

5. Be healthy

The challenging thing about priorities is not listing them, but honoring them. Like most married men I decreed my marriage more important than my work. If it ever came to choosing, I'd honor my wife every time. While that's not a choice one has to make daily, it's good to have it worked out in your mind (because it *will* happen). After all, deciding what to do when the doorbell rings would be mighty awkward without clear priorities to guide your thinking.

 Find a cemetery

Living by priorities (see #37) doesn't come naturally. The need of the moment pulls too hard. I'm the type of guy who can leave home focused and arrive at work scattered. Is this true in your life? Without constant realignment I'm ineffective. That's why I found a cemetery.

My cemetery sits a mile from our church and features a winding lane circling the grounds. This place has come to symbolize my walk with God. I've met Him there at all hours of the day and night, and at every stage along the emotional spectrum. I've cried, laughed, praised, and pleaded. I've also startled hundreds of creatures with my presence. I do life with God in that place. And it's a good thing, because a day or two without God-time is disastrous for me. I can create false gods overnight and serve them at a moment's notice. For me, daily time with God is mandatory.

In my cemetery I am reminded which of us is God and which is not. I explore His character, enjoy His presence, and rest in His care. It's where I go to experience who He is—which is a terrific teaser for what life will one day be. I not only talk out loud but I listen carefully. After all, it's a place where no amount of glitter can hide the obvious. Gravestones.

Your place doesn't have to be a cemetery. Study the history of God's people and you'll find quiet gardens, country roads, private closets, and drafty cells. A friend of mine favors a daily run through the woods. Jesus Himself sought lonely places where He could meet with His Father. The important thing is to find a place and spend the time.

Whatever set of priorities you come up with, God must be first, most, and always.[7] In youthwork, whether you're a parent, volunteer, or full-timer, living a life worthy of imitation is everything.[8] Without a genuine life, our words and example are insincere. And kids can smell hypocrisy at a thousand yards.

39 Manage your time, don't let it manage you

Learning to align activities with priorities is just as important as setting priorities in the first place. It means the difference between effectiveness and burnout. Though parents and volunteers don't experience this as much, full-time youthworkers have large blocks of discretionary time on their hands. Knowing how to use that time is key. Time management seminars put it this way:

Living in conflict with your values drains energy, whereas living in congruence with your values produces energy.

This golden nugget is worth a year's salary. Let's say I start the day with thirty-five items on my "to do" list. As I glance through the list I experience a range of emotions. Urgency, excitement, boredom, anxiety, dread, and so on. What am I likely to do first? The dreaded items? No way! I like adrenaline and excitement. Bring on the urgent tasks!

The problem is, urgency and excitement rarely coincide with value and priority. But they certainly generate energy! That's why they must be *harnessed* to move me through the higher priority jobs that lay before me. For example, notice how the tasks on the following list affect me:

Energy Drain	Energy Boost
Prepare a lesson	Check an item on eBay
Secure volunteers for a trip	Fix a conversation that didn't go well last night
Schedule an appointment with a hard-to-reach student	Deposit a check and grab lunch with a friend
Plan briefing for board meeting	Buy the latest gadget
Find a bus driver for an overnight event	Practice a few songs with the youth worship band
Confront a parent	Scope a trip location
Write a glowing reference for a student's college application	Tweak our website

If these items were to appear randomly on my list, I would naturally tackle the "energy" items first—arrive at work, check eBay, fix last night's awkward conversation, make some calls about our upcoming trip, check eBay again, make a few more calls about our trip, do some email, head for the bank, grab lunch with my friend, hit the Apple Store, add my cool ideas to our website, then run through a few numbers with the worship band. Suddenly it's 5:30 and I'm out the door for a quick supper before small group.

The trouble is, nothing important happened, and now I'm facing a tough tomorrow packed with heavy assignments. How much better to pick an important task, work it till 9:30, then toss in a booster. After that, tackle another important item until "lunch with a friend." And so on. Always harness your energy to pull you through what's important. Otherwise you'll never be in the mood even if you do find the time.

When it comes to discretionary time, here are several principles I've observed over the years:

- The important items on my list are the ones I will put off till "a better time."

- Tackling the urgent and exciting items first robs me of energy and time.

- Raw emotion is rarely in line with high priority.

- Accomplishing one or two highly significant items often yields an explosive energy for the rest of my list.

- Half of my time spent on important items usually yields enough margin for twenty or thirty nonimportant items.

How you spend your time says as much about your priorities as how you guard your heart or invest in your spiritual growth. Never make the mistake of thinking you are managing your time just because you plow through your list. In fact, if this routinely happens you should consider it a red flag. Few important tasks can be handled rapidly, especially in youthwork. And when the measure of accomplishment is young people learning to follow Christ, the discipline of effectiveness is worth the cost.

 ## If you're a full-time youthworker, pick an "All Day Home Day"

Right next to our front door is a large, vertical window. It stands as tall as the door and brings loads of light into the house. It also lets us look out.

I have an image of that window forever burned into my mind. In my early days of working with youth, our kids were very young. Each day when I'd leave for work, they would line up at that window. I'll never forget seeing their three faces pressed against the glass. Whether happy or streaked with tears, those faces were always there, watching and waiting.

They were waiting for what my toddler son dubbed "All Day Home Day".

You see, before I had kids of my own, an older youthworker told me to devote one day each week to my family. He was a seasoned veteran who had been through everything, so I figured he knew what he was talking about. At his suggestion I took every Thursday off. The phone went unanswered and my attention was undivided.

Now, more than twenty years later, I stare every new youthworker in the eyes and say the same thing. What's more, I've told leaders in other churches to mandate it for their youthworkers. Why? Because those years are short. There are only a few preschool years when you can be with your children all day. Then there are a few pre-adolescent years when you get them for half a day. Then there are a few adolescent years when you get to join them for breakfast at six in the morning. The years go fast and the solid foundation of your commitment to your family must be communicated early and clearly. Your kids need to know where they stand in your list of priorities. This is one of those things that matters a lot.

41 If you're a volunteer, pick an "All Day Home Day"

Let's say you're a parent or a volunteer. You log fifty to sixty hours a week at work and use Saturday to catch up on chores. Then comes Sunday. Church day. Chances are you're serving in some capacity at the church *and* working with the youth. When is your "All Day Home Day"?

Most volunteers don't get one. So be careful. Here are three things to consider if the previous paragraph describes you:

- Make sure your own kids know they come first. How will they know? Time together is a good place to start.

- Remember the most valuable thing you bring to the table when working with youth is yourself. Who you are. Your walk with Christ and love for His people. Make sure you are serving from a well-fed soul. Abide first, bear fruit as a result.

- Don't be afraid to say no. God has more than one arrow in His quiver. There are times for faithful service and times for faithful abstinence. There's much to be said for margin.

I've seen wise choices in this area yield enhanced fruitfulness later on. I've also seen God raise up others to take the place of those who need to invest at home. After all, He equips each member for the good of the community (Ephesians 4:16). Don't skimp at home to serve at church.

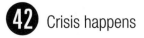 Crisis happens

One Thursday (my "All Day Home Day"), following a quick cafeteria lunch with my daughter, I stopped by the tool department at Sears. (I look for every excuse to stop there.) As I stood in line, happily clutching a long-awaited purchase, my cell phone rang. This surprised me. After so many years of honoring my "All Day Home Day," no one ever calls on Thursday. Juggling my package I glanced at the caller ID and saw it was my wife.

Within one second I realized something was wrong. Her voice was strained and I could tell she was crying. A man from our church had just died of a heart attack while running. He was a leader, well-liked, and respected. He had a large family and invested heavily in our young people. He was a close friend. *And he was my age.* Very quickly I returned the tool to its spot on the shelf and rushed to the home of my friend.

Now remember how I just finished proclaiming that you should jealously protect one day each week for your family? How I advised not answering the phone or checking email? That's all true.

Except when there's a crisis.

Crises seldom arrive with advanced warning and rarely at a good time. But when they come, our role as shepherds requires us to give 100 percent. That means instant response with no second thoughts. This is why living by priorities is so important. The person who is disciplined can adjust to temporary imbalances because he has invested in what's important. He has learned that crisis is the exception to the rule.

On the other hand, for the person who lives by the need of the hour, every day brings new crises. Over time, the boundaries between life, ministry, and emergency disappear. Though adrenaline can bring a surge of productivity, a constant run of it leads to burnout, damaged relationships, and lost opportunities. It's only when you make small, consistent investments in your priorities that you can borrow against them without guilt or fear.

Get organized

One thing you might have noticed at youthworker conventions is the staggering diversity of organizational tools. Some carry handheld gadgets that do more than a room full of early NASA computers. Others carry leather notebooks so massive they have to be checked as luggage on the plane. Then there are those who write on their hands. But everyone has some system because we all need help with human nature.

Human nature deals with things as they come and arranges tasks according to appetites (ambition, pleasure, fear, affirmation, and so on). Neither of these options will help you achieve your goals. Though it takes time, you'll be better served in the long run if you keep certain things in front of you. For example, my daily planner provides me with the following resources:

- Long-range goal lists

- Daily task lists

- A record of my values and priorities

- My schedule for the day

- Important business records

- Calendars

- Notes and ideas

Keeping these things in focus is a nonnegotiable tool in the hands of every effective youthworker—full-time or volunteer. Especially those of us with a strong relational bent. Why? *Because organization enables you to transfer your priorities into accomplishments.* It allows you to be effective, productive, and faithful.

There's a good word for this. It's *congruence* (see #39). When your daily choices reflect the things you value most, your behavior matches your convictions. Another word that comes to mind is *integrity*. Harmony between what you believe and what you do. Your daily planner (or iPhone or pocket full of notes or whatever you use) should help you live a priorities-driven life.

44 If you share the load, your students will thrive

Several summers ago one of our men took me out on his new sailboat. An experienced sailor myself, I showed up expecting to crew, but he insisted I sit and relax. Instinctively, I kept getting up to help, and he kept telling me to have a seat.

We passed through the seaway from Harbor Towne and hit the big lake, sailing all morning to reach a quaint little harbor in Macatawa for a late lunch. (Actually, *he* sailed. I watched.) As we approached the dock *under full sail* I noticed several picnic tables full of boaters. I noticed them because they had stopped eating and were gesturing toward our boat. The closer we got, the more they sat transfixed on our speed. Finally, when ramming the dock seemed unavoidable, several men jumped up and began shouting orders. Just then my host sprang to action. With uncanny speed he dropped sail, leapt across the boat, kicked bumpers over the side, and tossed a line around a dock cleat from aft our boat. The vessel stopped so abruptly I was thrown from my seat and could hear people cry out in alarm.

With the entire marina staff and all the restaurant guests staring at us, my host proudly exclaimed, "What did you think of that? Pretty amazing, huh?" He was beaming. I was looking for my cell phone to call a cab.

Whatever your comfort level with delegation, it's a "must" in youth ministry. It's the only way to ensure spiritual growth and development in your group, church, and self. If you're a full-time youthworker, delegation is your responsibility because it allows you to sustain your vision, extend your influence, and develop maturity in others. Watching others become skilled in ministry multiplies your effectiveness and is one of the priceless joys of youthwork.

It was hard for me to learn this. After all, I had lots of energy so it was easy to do all the work. And I like things done MY WAY. Besides, I felt guilty asking for help, assuming it made me look lazy. But God moved me through those hindrances because they kept others from what He wanted them to do. And it's only because others have invested that we've been able to shepherd thousands of young people over the years.

There are plenty of people in your fellowship who would love to invest in the lives of young people. They're just waiting for you to ask. Don't make them watch you do all the work—share it with them and watch your students thrive.

45 Be on the same page as your spouse

I've been told I'll never be fired—not because *I'm* doing such a great job, but because they don't want to lose my wife's contribution to the ministry. They've got that right!

This raises an important issue. Many churches view married youthworkers as two-for-the-price-of-one specials. Hire one youth-worker and get the spouse for free! Now *that's* good stewardship.

I'm not passing judgment on this perspective; I am throwing up a huge caution. Make sure you and your spouse are of one mind regarding your multiple roles with the group. Whether you work as a team, as gifted individuals, or one of you not at all, agree between yourselves what God is calling you to do. And if you're taking a new job, make sure the church knows what you've decided.

If you work with youth long enough, you'll pass through several phases of partnership. Young couples often have adequate margin to share. Conversely, jobs, pregnancies, children, and even inter-personal tensions can limit that margin. Julie and I worked together in the beginning, then took a fifteen year break while she invested full-time in our family. Now we're doing more together again and loving it.

Whatever your story, be aware of your situation, talk through the issues, and agree to honor your spouse whatever the circumstances. It is so important to be *proactive* in having these conversations with your spouse and your ministry staff.

 Fight the fatigue factor

We were laughing so hard we could barely hold the camera still. Six youthworkers absolutely covered in mud. Following our intense planning session, we'd taken to the woods on ATVs. Dirt, water, trees, brush, and laughter—the perfect balm for burnout.

One of the great things about youthwork is built-in recreation. To be sure, responsibility adds weight to running trips, retreats, and events, but the adventure and variety can be refreshing.

Yet such refreshment wears thin. As the years pile up the recreational aspect of youthwork fails to bring restoration. For example, a friend recently made fun of me for complaining about an upcoming "senior sneak" trip to the Abaco Islands. Exhausted by the prep work, I responded with the following testy email:

> *Yeah, this is a real vacation for me. Convincing the bank to give me $3,500 in fives and singles for taxi and ferry fees, renting six houses, six golf carts, two power boats, and one sailboat for a week, collecting 120 signed parent letters and sixty birth certificates (including the ones that don't exist), packing five guitars, one drum set, forty-five sets of snorkel gear, five coolers full of meat, and fifty-eight boxes full of food (Yes, officer, I packed it myself. No, officer, I don't know what's in it). Then there are the five different flights from two different cities on two different days (both ways), luggage restrictions of thirty-four pounds per girl (including carry-on bags) with each girl calling six times*

begging for more weight, zero tolerance for alcohol without being legalistic, and twelve of us with no place to sleep except on the boats because there are no more available rooms on the island. Yup, a real vacation.

The longer you stay in youthwork, the more important restoration and refreshment become. Working with people is fatiguing —even for "people persons." Ten-hour days, late-night activities, mile-long callback lists, and an endless schedule of difficult appointments will drain your strength. Then what?

Over the past few years I've been surprised by my desire to be alone. Always the "life of the party" type, I'd now be relieved never to see another party. These days, my favorite free time activity is working on cars. And with our fleet of aging vehicles, I get plenty of opportunity. For instance, here's what a typical Thursday morning now looks like for me:

• Decide which car needs fixing

• Unscrew something black with oil

• Attach something shiny and new

• Step back and admire my work with satisfaction

Playing with tools and machines is great fun for me. It's not a "have to," it's a "get to." If it ever grows burdensome I'll find some other way to recreate. But for now, mechanical work in a non-people environment restores my soul.

What about you? How do you regain lost strength? Even the hard-working, no-nonsense saints of yesteryear like George Mueller, Hudson Taylor, and Henrietta Mears broke from their grueling routines to refresh their souls. And many of their greatest ministry advances were rooted in those times of restoration. It's a practice I strongly recommend.

47 Don't forget how fast life happens

The most striking thing about growing older is observing the pace of change. Remember how it used to feel looking forward to something? Remember how long it took to come? For me it was getting my license and getting married. Each one felt like it took an eternity to arrive.

After a while, time becomes relative. It still slows down when I'm looking forward to something, but not as much. And once the "big day" or "big thing" arrives, time accelerates exponentially.

This is what happens with life.

When you enter your years of investment—like starting a family, for example—it's all-consuming and time stands still. But suddenly they pass, and you're left with the fruit of your investment.

Do you remember my "All Day Home Day" story about leaving for work with three little kids pressing their faces against the window? Do you know who looks out that same window now as the cars drive away?

I do.

My kids are no longer focused on Dad. They have spouses, jobs, college friends, groups, games, dates . . . and lives of their own.

Life changes. But you can be ready for it. Whether you're just beginning to work with young people or have been at it for years, take time to prioritize your life. That way, as its speed increases and the stages fly by, you will look back with joy and not regret. That's how you want it to be when you're the only one left at the window. ●

take **trips**

I grew up on trips. Why? Because my father didn't like what culture was doing to his family. He didn't oppose Little League, youth group, piano lessons, or neighborhood friends. He objected to the pace of our lives pulling us apart.

So he did something radical. He pulled his wife and kids out of all summer activities and hit the road. We got to bring our sleeping bags and one grocery sack full of used books each.

This was not good news. My brothers and I loved sports and dreamed constantly of making the big play. The thought of missing our teams that summer was almost unbearable. I can still taste the bitterness as I write this sentence. Dad's ratings in the polls hit rock bottom as we backed out of the driveway for the summer.

But then a remarkable thing happened. As we made our way west in a converted milk truck, we began to build memories together. While hiking down into the Grand Canyon we balanced on the outside edge of the trail when the mule trains lumbered by. We saw bear in Yellowstone, cliff-jumped in Yosemite, and gaped at the lights in Las Vegas.

I'll never forget reading by the campfire each night next to my dad. Every chapter was some new adventure—Chip Hilton saving the big game, or Tyrell Sackett drawing a hair quicker than the fastest outlaw in the West. My dad had this big old book that took up too much space in our crowded milk truck, so every time he'd finish a page he'd tear it out of the book and toss it into the fire. Is it any wonder I love reading?

I experienced six major trips with my family ranging from six to ten weeks each. We spent time in every corner of the country, including Alaska. During one of those trips I realized what my father was doing. When we left town that summer (one minute after the final school bell), an older boy named Davey was standing on the street corner in the middle of our town. I waved at him. Two months later as we drove back into town I remember saying to my dad, "Hey look! There's Davey. He's standing in the same place he was when we left!" That's when it dawned on me. We'd just experienced a world of adventure, and all that time Davey had been standing still.

Can you hear the momentum in my words? Can you picture just how small Little League had become in my mind? Can you imagine the wealth of perspective those trips brought to my work, life, and relationships the rest of the year? They shaped who I am today.

The same can be true for your youth. Expose them to God, His creation, and other cultures. Let them taste risk. Reset their relational context as often as you can. Run trips—lots of them! And watch the life of God pour in through the windows you create.

 Build momentum

Some youthworkers love 'em while others hate 'em, but few question their value. Trips deliver! They throw off massive momentum and strengthen community among young people.

Our culture is awhirl in converging factors that make trips both attractive and potent. Consider the following trends:

- Our culture values experience. Students don't want to hear about adventure, they want to taste it.

- The speed of culture has robbed most students of meaningful relationships. This creates relational hunger.

- Factors that build relationships include spending time together and sharing memories.

What pays higher dividends in each of these categories than being on a trip with someone else? The higher the dividend, the greater the momentum.

One year we had our graduating seniors gather on the platform to share what they valued most from their time in the youth group. Ninety percent of them referenced a trip. And all the middle schoolers in the room couldn't wait till it was their turn.

49 Shared experience bonds students

Relational compression has to do with increasing the pace at which relationships develop. You get to determine this pace based on how you design your trips. For instance, let's say you run a trip from Chicago to the Tennessee mountains: You've got forty students and five adults. During the planning stage you explore two options for transportation—renting three fifteen-passenger vans or hiring a forty-seven passenger bus.

The vans will be cheaper, but the bus will yield greater relational compression. Why? Because all forty-five of you will experience the same thing. By the end of the trip you'll share one set of travel jokes, one memory of the backed-up toilet, and one gasp at the hairpin turn near the top of Mountainside Drive. *Shared experience bonds students,* and you get to help make that happen.

Here's another example. Based on my experience, I think boats deliver the highest payoff in relational compression. For one thing, you can determine how often you put into port. Fewer stops equals more compression. On one of our trips students crew the boats through several forty-hour segments. During that time they work together in tight quarters, depend on each other for safety, and—since they have no other choice—resolve conflict together. Talk about compression!

Want even more relational payoff? Minimize technology (cell phones, iPods, gaming devices, etc.). Eliminate everything that adds layers, walls, barriers, or distance, and then watch what happens.

Create new opportunities

As you plan events and trips begin, to see all the "secondary" opportunities that exist for relationship building. Maybe you're setting up a mission trip. While *serving* would likely be your top goal, *relational growth* is also crucial to the spiritual growth of your students. You can find plenty of it if you know where to look. For example:

- **Lodging**—Kids love the closeness of lodging environments. Sometimes they love it too much! No matter—you can easily harvest the dynamic and still stay one step ahead of them in terms of appropriate behavior.

- **Meeting places**—Be creative in selecting where you meet. Think about the surroundings—distractions, smells, views. Even the lighting! Does the room assault you with a blazing florescent glare radiating off four bleach-white walls? Look for something better. Some of our best meetings have taken place in stairways where the acoustics elevated our worship in ways we never would have imagined.

- **Transportation**—As mentioned earlier, this can significantly impact relational growth. During one extremely demanding trip to Mexico (forty hours each way), I had seven adults arguing with each other over who the good drivers were and who had no business being on the road. In other words, we had seven vans transporting seven divided youth groups.

- **Special event**—Insert a treat in the middle of your trip. Surprise fireworks at night, a water park on a hot day, hiking up to a waterfall, or even a restaurant upgrade can add the needed touch at the right time.

I could go on and on—relational treasures are buried everywhere. It's our job to harness their yield for the sake of our students.

51 Plan trips based on group goals

We define trips by their underlying purpose. We've been to Jamaica for missions and to its neighbor, the Dominican Republic, for a senior reward trip. Though the climate and scenery were similar, our purpose and activities were different. Both yielded invaluable payoff, yet we justified, publicized, and paid for them in totally different ways. We also prayed for them differently. The point is: Trips are a useful tool for many of your primary group goals.

Here's a sample list of trips with varying purposes we've run during the past couple of years:

Trip	Environment	Purpose
Dawntreader	Sailing	Spiritual growth
Mexico	Developing region	Service & evangelism
Isle Royale	Backpacking	Leadership development
DC/LA	Conference	Evangelism training
Snowriders	Snowboarding	Outreach
Teton Wilderness	Mountains	Small group development
Ace Whitewater	Outdoor	Adventure
Senior Sneak	Caribbean	Stage of life / Transitions

52 Slash those prices

One of the primary factors in running trips is keeping costs down. Way down. And the best way I know to do that is to **avoid per person costs whenever possible**! There. Have I given that enough emphasis?

Sometimes they're unavoidable. It's hard to fly anywhere without paying per seat. But you should still work around per person pricing *every time you can*. Organizations that charge by the person are usually covering overhead. Why should your students pay for someone else's salary? Why not create your own programs?

Here's an example. Every summer we run a world-class sailing trip in the North Channel of Lake Huron for less than $500 per person. How? By leasing boats for a set fee per boat (bareboating). If a boat costs $2,000 for the week and is set up to sleep six adults, we put twelve on it. That way I can whack my student's costs from $333 per person to $166. We're in youth work, right? We're not about creature comforts—we're about relational compression and spiritual development.

There are loads of trips out there that can be run cost-effectively. How much does it really cost to backpack, bike, canoe, or tube?

Here's another example. Our Mexico trips are designed to donate at least 70 percent of student costs to the local churches where we work, yet we only charge students $450 for this trip. We pull this off by driving the forty hours to Torreon, Mexico, and packing our travel food. While in Mexico we sleep on the floor of a church, eat what the people feed us, and work sunrise to sunset every day. And we explain all this to our church before we go, noting the degree to which we're willing to sacrifice and challenging them to cover our transportation costs. It's a win-win.

Each year in Mexico we donate around $8,000 of our student trip fees. The local churches use this money to purchase block, cement, windows, and other materials for their church buildings. When all is said and done we're running a cost-effective trip, teaching kids how to serve, and making a kingdom difference in Mexico.

A little creativity can go a long way on a trip.

53 Make it as easy as possible on your adult volunteers

When adults get excited about running trips, it multiplies effectiveness. Actually, it multiplies *everything*. For instance, excited adults mean:

- The trip has instant credibility with parents.

- The work of planning the trip is shared as adults *anticipate* the trip by working together.

- The old problem of drumming up adult support turns into a new problem . . . too many adults.

- Delegation happens. Once you start running trips, leaders rise to the surface. Even though our church has full-time youth pastors, many of our large trips are planned and run by volunteer adults.

- Marketing takes care of itself as parents spread the word to other parents and kids pick up on the anticipation.

Whenever possible we don't charge our adults. Rather, we build the cost of their involvement into the trip. Obviously it's not possible to always do this, but we do it every time we can. Why?

- An adult is most likely sacrificing vacation time to come on the trip.

- An adult is not going to get much sleep while on the trip.

- That means they'll most likely return worn out.

Imagine communicating the above reality to them and then saying, "By the way, you owe me $500 for this privilege." It just doesn't seem right. It's not that trips are hard—many adults come home as spiritually refreshed and charged up as the kids! They're away from their normal cares and responsibilities, everything is planned and provided, the camaraderie is rich, and they experience the same spiritual input as the students. I've had countless adults tell me the trips they attend are annual high points. It's just that volunteers are usually making a sacrifice to come, so we honor that by reducing their cost when we can.

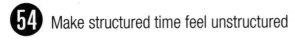
54 Make structured time feel unstructured

How much structure should you build into your trips? That depends. Some schedules should be highly developed so every moment counts. Others should involve structure as a last resort. Here are several factors to consider before planning a schedule:

- What age group are you working with? Younger students need more structure. They benefit from it and self-destruct without it.

- A blend of structured and unstructured times works well.

- Flexibility and structure also work well together. A group of leaders often have good collective intuition about what needs to happen next. Perhaps a meeting should be cancelled in favor of one-on-one dialogue. Or maybe the free time block is too large and students aren't handling it well. Keep some options up your sleeve.

- We schedule "guided discretionary time" with older students. For example, "This next hour is designed for you to pursue each other with one of the following questions . . ." (Questions might include: What is one goal you have for the coming school year? How has it been going with your friends lately? When and where was the last God-sighting in your life?)

- Make structured time feel unstructured. That is, plan things so your students have choices and are responsible to honor them. Even though some will not take it seriously, those who do will improve their skills in using time wisely.

- Schedule a daily slot for devotions or personal quiet time. This takes the pressure off students trying to find time on their own.

 **Put safety first**

I could write a book on this topic alone. Get it right and your options multiply tenfold. When it comes to getting places, I always consider three things:

- Safety

- Costs

- Efficiency

As far as *safety* goes, I'll never forget one particular night when I would rather have been in bed with the flu than dealing with the situation unfolding before my bleary eyes. It was 2:30 in the morning and I had a fight on my hands. *A fight between two adults.*

We were somewhere between Michigan and Florida and I had a purple-faced man shouting at full volume, "I'm not getting back in that van if you let her drive!" The woman he referred to was locked in the bathroom doing what all mature adults do at that hour—crying hysterically and refusing to come out.

Behind us were four vans loaded with kids and not enough experienced drivers to cover three shifts per van. And make no mistake—you really do need three good drivers when facing a twenty-six-hour haul. (Twenty-six hours without stopping for fights, that is.) I hadn't rounded up enough veteran drivers so I sprinkled some in from my "Reserves" list. Unfortunately, there are power drivers and timid drivers, and the two don't mix.

That trip pushed me over the edge. We now take buses to Florida.

We've done trips with cars, vans, motorhomes, buses, and other "vehicles" I'd rather not even mention. Nearly anything with wheels will get you there, but don't overlook safety as you make your decision. Always ask these questions:

- Can the trip be handled in ten hours or less?

- Will the trip involve driver fatigue factors (lack of sleep, noise, heat, young students, cities, mountains)?

- How experienced are my drivers? Am I working with twentysomethings or seasoned adults?

- What's my budget? Am I building enough transportation costs into what I'm charging the students?

- What's available in my area?

- How large is my group? Complexity increases with group size.

One day last summer I was driving down a stretch of interstate near our house. Traffic was backed up for miles. Sitting on the guardrail with gloom and dejection written all over their faces were a mom, dad, and three kids. Nearby sat their crunched SUV attached to their wrecked travel trailer. Instantly I felt sad. All those weeks and months of expectations dashed in one wrong move. A summer of disappointment, not to mention expense.

Thankfully, no one appeared hurt, but their trip was ruined. So it is with *safety*. Do your best to minimize the risks through wise choices and careful planning.

56 Don't go anywhere without prayer

"The best laid plans of mice and men often go awry . . ." so don't just depend on good planning. Make sure people are praying. Have your congregation begin months before each trip, and get the students praying for each other. We've even had people praying around the clock while we're gone, using our trip itineraries to guide their prayers.

We don't go anywhere without strong and continuous prayer support. Don't leave home without it.

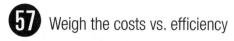

57 Weigh the costs vs. efficiency

To understand how *costs* and *efficiency* work together, consider the following options:

Option	Advantages	Disadvantages
Car	Free (usually) Readily available Easy to find drivers	Limited sizes requires more vehicles (higher fuel costs) as group grows More drivers means greater risk
Motorhome	Comfortable Bathroom saves stops Prepare and serve food while you drive	Expensive to rent Not very safe Things break easily
Van	Cheapest per person seat cost Easy and affordable to rent Affordable to purchase Easy and affordable to maintain Can pull trailers	The larger the group the more drivers needed Most van drivers are not professionals or even experienced No bathroom means more stops Seating configuration not very relational
Bus	*. . . on following page*	

Option	Advantages	Disadvantages
Bus	Experienced drivers	Requires qualified drivers
	Shared experience for larger groups	Expensive to own and maintain
	Bathroom saves time	Expensive to rent
	Mobility during travel	Not versatile in tight quarters
	Bunks provide break for second driver	

Clearly, the size of your group will point you toward a solution. Still, it's important to know and weigh the options. Our group has gone the bus route. Because of the ongoing dip in the bus market, the purchase price of an older bus is actually comparable to a van (though the upkeep is more demanding).

With a bus you can enjoy the benefits of experienced drivers, greater safety, and relational compression. And if other churches in your area also own buses, you can organize co-ops and share them. We've done this for years.

On the other hand, I only recommend the bus option if you regularly find yourself renting more than three vans. Running one to three vans on a trip is quite reasonable. Running four or more puts me in the red zone.

Here's a good trick for evaluating options—*ask yourself how you can avoid the last two hours of your trip.* We know the most dangerous hours for hauling students come at the end of a trip when drivers are tired and passengers are antsy to get home. How can you trim your travel to avoid unnecessary time? Consider the following suggestions:

- Limit stops. Twenty-five people stopping for almost anything will always take more time than you think.

- Pack food to eat on board. This will save you an hour.

- If you can't pack your own food, order takeout from 25 minutes away with a cell phone. Swing in, have two people offload for the food, and you're on your way in ten minutes.

- Travel with vehicles that have bathrooms.

- Never use gas station bathrooms. Use rest areas. If you have thirty or more people on a trip and you stop at a gas station, here's what happens. There's usually one seat per gender. So everyone stands around. Especially the guys since the line for the girl's room is a mile long. Pretty soon they're all shopping, buying giant slurpies and two-liter bottles of soda (because they're a good deal, Don). This guarantees another stop in one hour, just after you've finally loaded everyone back on the bus from this stop. Believe it or not, you can stop at a rest area for the bathrooms *and* a gas station for fuel (with students staying on board) in less time than it takes to do both at the same gas station.

Some of this may sound extreme, but when you consider how strenuous those last two hours of a long trip are, it's worth preserving the safety and spirit in which people return home.

Dream outside the box

You can spin endless variations with trips. That means almost any trip can be made uniquely yours. Our best ideas are the ones we dream up as a team, but you don't need a team to give your trips a distinctive edge. Here are some tips for making that happen:

- **Collect and store pieces of the puzzle**—For example, I've always been intrigued by trains. I think being on a train would create a great dynamic between kids and leaders, so I collect ideas, prices, and stories, and let them simmer on the back burner.

- **Beat the system**—I know I could buy a great trip for a million dollars, but I don't want to. So I collect ideas that are cheap. Just recently a guy told me about some ferry that hauls groups from Seattle to Alaska for a nominal fee. In fact, the passengers camp right on the deck of the ship. As he was talking I heard my key word—*cheap*—and wrote it down!

- **Dream outside the box**—What's something that would be bigger, better, and more expensive than you can afford? Write it down, tweak it, and figure out the angles. I'll bet you can bring it in for way less than you think.

Even though we already have an extensive trip program, we're still dreaming. The current trip forming in my mind includes the following components:

- Amtrak from Chicago to Glacier National Park

- Backpack Glacier for a couple of days

- Amtrak from Glacier to Seattle

- Ferry to Alaska

- Whales and eagles by the score

Although this trip is not yet official, I know it will be a success. Why? Because it's huge and unique! And when I'm done with it, it'll also be *cheap*.

Out of the box doesn't have to mean out of state

Getting kids out of their local context and giving them a new perspective can be quick and easy.

Know someone in a nearby city? Take your group there for a sleepover. One of my best friends from college pastors a church in Chicago—a mere four hours from us. More than once I've loaded our students into vans (or a bus!) and hauled them to the other side of the lake for a cross-cultural reality check. You can accomplish plenty in forty-eight hours with two bus rides, a gym, deep dish pizza, and urban engagement. All for the price of some gas. (The kids buy their own pizza—most high school kids can scrounge up ten bucks when they want to.)

60 Make T-shirts

Identity is huge and T-shirts proclaim it. That's why we budget for T-shirts on every trip. Some students collect them while others wear them to shreds. I love scanning a crowded gym and seeing scores of T-shirts from our different groups, trips, and events.

Sometimes we design them, but just as often we have students do it. Either way, T-shirts draw groups together and generate tons of energy. I've seen innumerable pictures of students wearing our T-shirts in other cities, states, countries, and continents. It may seem like a small thing, but the dividends far outweigh the costs. *Do T-shirts whenever you can.*

61 Where to find money for trips

Determining whether or not you can afford a trip is always a "half empty or half full" exercise. If your committee's cup is half empty, you'll probably not attempt the trip because it will seem beyond you.

If your cup is half full, you'll seem irresponsible to the half empty people, the bookkeeper, and possibly the board. But you'll also pull off some legendary trips and see lives changed.

I've been fascinated by what people can scrounge up on limited budgets. We've even run trips that cost over $1,000 per student several years running—and it's not because we have a budget that big.

If you believe in trips and what they can accomplish for you, then your operative word is *STRETCH*! Don't be imprisoned by the notion that you can't afford it.

So where does all this money come from? Most of the time it's the same three options:

- The student (or their parents) pays

- The church budget pays

- Fund-raising pays

Most of us use a combination of the above options. Check out the following hypothetical chart and the various percentages assigned to each type of trip:

	Mission	Adventure	Leadership
Students	60%	80%	50%
Budget	20%	0%	50%
Fund-raising	20%	20%	0%

Let's assume in the above example of a mission trip my total cost is $6,000 for fifteen people. I don't want to charge my students $400 per person because I don't think they can (or will) come up with it. Therefore, I lower their cost to $240 and supplement with

$1,200 from the church budget and $1,200 from fund-raising.

Notice my values in the above chart. I choose not to budget money for an adventure trip. But I heavily invest budgeted money for leadership development.

The word *fund-raising* doesn't always sit well with people. Lots of bad experiences have been had. However, many people enjoy donating to students, especially for life-changing causes. So don't write it off too quickly.

Within the fund-raising universe there are important factors to consider:

- Student time

- Adult time

- Target audience

- Per person or per hour financial yield

Let's be honest. The goal of fund-raising is to raise money. We're not investing our energy to run an activity or burn free time. Take a look at the following chart and consider the yields. Let's say you have ten students and two adults, plus some hidden costs . . .

Project	Student Time	Adult Time	Target Audience	$/Person Hour
Car wash	4 hours	7 hours	Random	$3.25
Corporate	4 hours	5 hours	Business	$7.50
Something -a-thon	4 hours	6 hours	Friends & relatives	$26.94

Let's break these examples down:

- **Car wash**—The adults find a good corner with lots of traffic. They also organize supplies, buy soap, and arrange for the business owner to donate water and a work space. Then they spend $20 on supplies and $40 on pizza for the kids. The kids, in between squirting each other, wash ten cars per hour and make $5 per car. Their overall take for the day is $200, which nets out to $3.25 per hour once you deduct expenses and average everyone's time. Never make the mistake of thinking you made $200. You didn't. You made $140 and put way too much time into it.

- **Corporate**—This type of fund-raiser is where we agree to work a project for some business. Businesses often host events where they need extra volunteers, or they just come up with something that needs to be done. We've done painting, roofing, cleaning, banquet setup, serving meals, child care, handing out programs and door prizes, window cleaning, event cleanup, and all sorts of other projects for businesses. Generally speaking, businesses are generous and donate far more than we're worth. We once sent fifteen students to do a four-hour job and the company donated $750. We didn't earn that much— they were just generous. They were also thinking in terms of an hourly rate per person, which is more than you get at a car wash.

- **Something-a-thon**—These are events where students collect pledges per hour or per increment. It's like "piece-work" and can yield a tremendous amount of money. The good thing about swim-a-thons, run-a-thons, or rake-a-thons is that the students do all the work. They collect the pledges and expend the energy. Our job is simply to remind them to collect their money once they are finished.

The cool thing about *something-a-thons* is that students can raise money according to their motivation. We've used this type of fund-raiser when running an adventure trip or something where we're passing most of the costs on to the students.

Let's say you want to run a whitewater-backpacking trip that will cost $500. Some students will ask their parents to write checks for the entire amount. Others will have no idea how to generate that much cash, *yet they really want to be on that trip.* This type of fund-raiser allows such a student to get busy. He can swim one hundred laps and get his friends to donate one cent per lap. That means a dollar per friend. But how many friends does he have? And what about coaches, band-directors, teachers, youthworkers, grandparents, neighbors, and employers? I've seen students make $500 per event simply because they needed to.

Considering the data, trips are affordable for nearly all of us regardless of the challenges we face. And once you pull one off, others will follow.

62 Join forces

At some point along the way you will either benefit from joining another already existing program or be asked if others might join you on an event or trip. For instance, when you take kids to a summer camp, you are piggy-backing on an established program.

We recently had an exciting time joining another group for a shared mission trip. We've been working with a community in Mexico for about ten years now. Formerly this consisted of us traveling there and putting dollars and man-hours into their ongoing work. However, we just did a joint project together that took our program to a new level. We have more financial resources, and this other group has more contact resources. So we joined forces. Their church sent a team of ten people to join our team at a new mission outpost. It was a fantastic experience that neither of us could have managed alone.

The benefits of joint experiences are:

- Small youth groups can offer more to their students.
- Larger groups can contribute vision and momentum to developing programs.
- Individuals can experience growth outside the confines of a limited program/their comfort zones.
- Large youth groups get a chance to see beyond themselves.
- Transportation benefits arise.
- Pricing can be more cost-efficient with increased numbers.

63 "Wherever we go, we go in Jesus' name"

Think about the biblical book of Acts. It describes trips. Trips that changed lives and altered the course of history. That's how I view trips. It's what I plan for, pray for, and prepare our group for. When we leave home we go in Jesus' name, whether it's a mission trip, leadership-training venture, or Senior Sneak. And by God's grace, it's sometimes our own students who find Him along the way.

How you view and discuss your trips sets the tone for how your church perceives them. Elders need to know what they're support-ing (or funding), and parents want to know what their children will be doing. Spiritual takeaway? Character growth? Cross-cultural experience? Danger? Your language, objectives, and the context you describe will set the tone for how trips are received—and often for how they deliver.

Remember my summer spent in the milk truck? I don't think

my dad ever used the word *vacation*. We had an adventure. We learned what life was like for other people. We discovered reality and learned to face it head on. And we encountered a God of grandeur and majesty.

The buses are standing by! ●

be **smart** with money

ONE Friday afternoon Jules and I realized we didn't have all the necessary ingredients for the Build Your Own Burrito Bash we were hosting that night. That meant a quick run to the store. Now there's a small, pricey store two blocks from our house, and a huge discount store six miles away. Not one to waste hard-to-find money I opted to save a few bucks at the six-mile store.

If there's one thing I love about grocery shopping, it's plastic bags. Unlike juggling paper sacks, you can now carry $500 worth of groceries in one load. Just hook a bag on each finger and waddle off like Santa Claus.

As I was leaving the store, I ran straight into two small boys. They were staring up at me, wearing Scout uniforms, and holding a large box of popcorn. This reminded me of three very important things:

1. I just drove six miles to save five bucks.
2. I'm holding ten bags of groceries.
3. I hate popcorn.

But you know what I did. I lowered my bulging bags to the cement—ignoring the items that began spilling out and rolling toward the parking lot—and reached deep into my pocket for ten dollars. It's not easy standing in the hot sun *on a Friday afternoon asking strangers for money, so I felt honored to support them in their small act of service. After all, I'd rather invest my money in kids than donate it to the corporate owners of an over-priced convenience store.*

Most of us don't realize how willing people are to invest in projects involving young people. Of all the giving opportunities people face, giving to youth remains near the top. Since finances play such a large role in enabling student ministry, keep this in mind when planning.

---

64 It's not fund-raising, it's harnessing interest

The term *fund-raising* has a bad rap. It makes people cranky and fearful. That's too bad, because adults love giving money to students. They also enjoy supporting tangible projects. So when you combine young people and purposeful events, you have a ripe field for harvest.

The key is in how you do it.

You'll find several tips on fund-raising for trips in chapter 6, so I'll merely offer an example here that can work for any type of fund-raising to make the point. We recently sponsored a two-week trip for our entire high school group combining a week of missions work with a week at a national youth conference. Rather than soliciting donations or having the students write letters to their relatives, we compiled a list of students who were available to do part-time work. One of the parents who does an excellent job with administration became our dispatcher, matching jobs from the congregation with students by geographical location. During the three months we ran this program, thousands of dollars poured in, directly to the students, from hundreds of church members. Many of our people looked for any possible excuse to hire students and give them money. *People love supporting students who are trying to live for God.* One woman hired a boy to move some boards from her car to the garage. She paid him the equivalent of sixty dollars an hour and sustained him with donuts, cookies, and milk. That beats writing letters if you ask me.

 View budgets in terms of students

When managed wisely, finances extend your ability to reach kids for the kingdom of God. It follows then that stretching your financial goals is a good thing, so long as your planning is sound. That's why budgets should grow over time.

Yet money is sticky business. Budgets are often tight and safeguards abound. It's not uncommon to hear statements like this:

> "Here's your budget for next year. Please be careful not
> to exceed your limit, and you'll need a second signature
> for any expense over fifty dollars."

Wow. That's like trying to ride a horse that's tethered to a tree. So how does one loosen the rope and amply provide for student discipleship? Here are a few tips we've learned over time.

First, as you communicate a budget to your board or accountability partners, shift the focus from money to people—especially when you're asking for an increase. Whenever I'm preparing budget spreadsheets, I always include dollar-per-student ratios. This will help you think efficiently (how to gain the most student influence per dollar in your checkbook): "It cost us $xx per student last year to bring them through our discipleship program. With the growth our group has experienced this year and the improvements we've made to increase our effectiveness, we're now looking at an overall savings of $x per student for the coming year."

This isn't just semantics. The more thinking you do in terms of dollars per student, the more opportunities you'll uncover to improve your program. (More on this a little bit later.)

The *second* thing to remember is that a budget is a guide. It is meant to communicate the priorities and direction of your program, not the untouchable arrangement of numbers in a list. I'm not suggesting you cast off restraint and chase all your dreams. Just make sure that the conversation always focuses on the meaning behind the money. Whether it's you talking to the elders or the elders addressing the congregation, acknowledge and honor the overall limits, but talk in terms of your goals and the gains you're making in achieving them. You may not see more dollars in your account, but you'll elevate the discussion and keep everyone focused on students rather than costs.

66 Paint a picture other people can see

It was eight months into the budget year and I was squirming. The board was combing through our financial statements and questioning each of us about our expenditures. I could not get comfortable in my chair.

When they began interrogating the pastor to my left because his budget was two hundred dollars overspent, I knew this wouldn't be pretty. Mine was six thousand in the red. What would I say? I could use the old "cash flow" trick where I blamed everything on a trip I'd paid for but not yet collected on.

Except I'd used that argument last month.

A trickle of sweat ran down my neck.

Then it was my turn and all eyes were on me. I opened my mouth . . . but nothing came out. I didn't know what to say. In the awkward silence that ensued, *it was one of the board members* who came to my rescue.

"How many students are you working with right now?" he asked. "And how does that number compare to the number at the beginning of the year?"

Thank you, Lord . . .

The fact is, elders have a tough job. Fiscal accountability is vital for good stewardship, yet shepherding students involves a certain fluidity. Reckless spending and rigid thinking are both bad. (At least in *my* opinion!) The board member who came to my rescue was thrilled by the surge of growth we were experiencing. He didn't care how much we'd overspent because kids were coming to faith and their families were showing up at church. And how did he know about such things? We'd discussed it over lunch three weeks earlier.

To those whose hearts favor other ministries, youthwork can seem like a runaway train—an out-of-control child needing restraint, not encouragement. But even people like that warm to the discovery that God is at work.

So paint a picture they can see.

67 Think in "dollars per student"

It's a mistake to make lump sum comparisons between budgets. For example, in 1983 our youth budget was $1,800. I was volunteering and we had five kids showing up. One weekend I drove to Detroit with a couple other youthworkers so we could meet with the youth director of a huge church. He had just taken the job, had 1,200 kids in his program, and was in the process of hiring six more youth pastors.

I was in awe. His budget was $175,000 per year and his trips seemed out of this world. However, as we broke it down by spending per person, things came clear. With five kids, $1,800 meant I was investing $360 in each student. Wow! *That's a lot of money!*

And what about the Detroit church? With 1,200 students in their program they were scraping by with a mere $145 per student. (I offered to loan them some money if they ever hit a rough spot.)

The bigger your program is the harder it becomes to maintain a healthy budget. That's why you'll want to keep ratios in mind as you plan and present your budgets. Ministering to young people in large groups can seem financially efficient, but it does not yield the same effect as investing personally in each one. And personal ministry involves time, which requires staffing, which means dollars. So remember the goal and describe your budgets relationally, not just with numbers (I've said this a few times now because it is so important).

68 Create clear categories

As your program grows you can avoid budgetary "sticker shock" by organizing your budget around multiple categories. We use the following categories in our student ministry budget:

- Transportation
- Vehicle Maintenance
- Student Ministries
- Youth Missions

What's nice about this breakdown is that the top two are simply fixed-cost items. Within reason, it's hard to overspend in those categories. Students need to be transported and vehicles need to be maintained. The board knows we're always looking for the best option on transportation, so they work with us on transportation costs. (Does this mean we always get what we want? Nope. You may need to make tough choices or sacrifice trips, but those decisions will be practical, not theoretical.)

This allows for more clarity on our high-value line items. Youth missions and student ministries become easier to assess when you back out the other stuff. Consider the following comparison:

- **Next Year's Budget:**

  Student Ministries – $136,000 . . . *or*

- **Next Year's Budget:**

  Transportation – $15,000

  Vehicle Maintenance – $12,000

  Student Ministries – $96,000

  Youth Missions – $13,000

When the conversation starts out $40,000 less than it might have, depending on how you present your information, it's easier to address the specific value of the actual ministry items you're proposing. Again, this is not about semantics or sleight of hand, but presenting your ministry plans in the clearest possible way. *Never underestimate clarity in communication.*

69 The resources are out there—go find them

There are valuable resources hidden right under your nose. No kidding. It's amazing what you can discover by poking around a bit in your own community (not just affluent communities, either). Resources abound when student development is the goal. For example:

- More than once the large automobile companies in Detroit have loaned us fifteen-passenger vans for an entire week free of charge. We've even taken some of them over the border into Mexico.

- One of our local food chains disburses checks to nonprofit groups based on a percentage of grocery tabs.

- Foundations in our area regularly donate significant chunks of money for work projects.

- Businesses that need temporary help can use youth groups for one-day projects.

- Work projects are plentiful within every community, especially in the spring.

- Fluctuations within the economy can provide occasional opportunities. Right now you'll find a glut of used coach buses on the market. Buses that would have set you back $60,000 five years ago can be purchased for less than $10,000 right now, and some may even be available as donations.

The point of all this? Resources are available for the taking. I happen to like digging up special deals, but not everyone does. If you do, great—I guarantee you'll find something worth knowing about.

But let's say you'd rather dig ditches than scrounge around looking for treasure. I'll bet there's someone in your church who would be thrilled to play such a part in your youth ministry. Ask around and pray for God's direction. He gifts all kinds of people with priceless abilities, and when the end result means blessing and encouraging the lives of your youth, there's no telling what they might come up with.

70 The resources are in your church—go find them

Stand in the back of your sanctuary next Sunday and look at all the people. Not as a crowd, but as uniquely gifted individuals. Those people have what your group needs. I've said this before, but it's true in several ways—and I'm not talking about fund-raising.

Here's a recent example. One year we planned a retreat and later discovered we couldn't run the entertainment options we'd counted on. What to do?

Set a bunch of guys loose on the problem, that's what.

One man knew a few things about salvage prices. Another was an expert at sniffing out automotive bargains. Someone else could hatch outrageous ideas at a moment's notice. By the time we ran the retreat, the purchasing expert had acquired a fleet of functional automobiles, the salvage expert had lined up their disposal for more money than we'd invested, and the idea man gave us more to do with those things than we had time for.

The result: *An unforgettable weekend retreat that generated a profit.* So remember—there's gold hidden in those pews (or chairs), and it's not just in people's wallets.

71 When it comes to need, show, don't tell

In our early days we had this brown van that was supposed to hold fifteen kids. It actually did fit fifteen, as long as none of them fell through the holes in the floor.

Over the course of a year we put ads in the bulletin and occasionally mentioned our need for a new van from the pulpit, but the money didn't come in. Finally, someone got the idea to simulate what it looks like to take a couple dozen students on a trip in a dilapidated van. The pastor let us have five minutes at the end of a service and we went for the jugular!

Using the actual seats from the van, we acted out a skit where twenty-seven young people tried to sit on seats built for fifteen. During the brief skit we demonstrated that students were:

• sitting on top of each other

- getting their feet caught in the floorboard holes

- taking their lives into their own hands by using an overcrowded van

We then took an offering and collected $12,000 on the spot—which, at that stage in the life of our church, was an unbelievable amount of money.

Kids communicate the vulnerability of adolescent development. Adults recognize this and support it, which is exactly as it should be. That's the role of adults—to watch over the young until they themselves are equipped as adults. Don't lose sight of this.

72 Equip your students to own the needs of the ministry

In the opening story of this chapter about the Boy Scouts, there was a scoutmaster standing behind the table. The two boys, however, were out front. They were the ones approaching every person leaving the store.

If the scoutmaster had asked for money I could easily have turned him down. "Sorry, my friend. My hands are full, and I already donate to a number of worthy causes."

But could I turn down two boys looking up at me with that special, fragile look? Are you kidding? There's no way I'm going to crush those impressionable young spirits.

It's important to keep students in front of adults. Adults need to experience the grace of empowering young people to find their way and gain strength in the faith. Besides, nothing makes an adult feel better than firsthand experience with "It is better to give than to receive." ●

be prepared for **deviance**

PRETEND you're sitting at a coffee shop with a sophomore. His brow is furrowed, and he keeps checking to see who just came in. Small talk isn't going well and dinner at home starts in forty-five minutes. If you had invited him you'd be thinking, "Okay, maybe next time." But you didn't. He asked you to be there. Said he needed to talk with you. Except he's not talking.

"So Chad, what's on your mind?"

"Oh man, I am in big trouble," he blurts.

He's sweating and won't look you in the eyes. Something's seriously wrong, and even though he picked you to tell, he can't get it out.

"Tell me about it."

Out it comes. "Stacy came over last night so we could do algebra together. That's all!"

His eyes hit the floor. "So, like then my mom comes barging in without knocking, and we weren't even going to do anything! I mean, we were talking about it not being right and were putting our clothes back on and . . ."

Oh my. These kids are leaders in the group. Model students with great parents. Stacy leads a group and Chad is on the tech crew.

What will you say?

What questions run through your mind?

What should you tell the parents? Should you talk it over with one of the pastors?

Kids today don't just do "algebra" with their girlfriends. Few even have girlfriends—that's old school. Nowadays everything happens in groups, and the damage runs deep and wide:

> *"The heart is more deceitful than all else*
> *And is desperately sick;*
> *Who can understand it?"* (Jeremiah 17:9 NASB).

Deviance is in the heart. It pollutes, poisons, and destroys. As culture sheds morality, there are no restraints. And young people pay the price. If you work with youth you know what I'm talking about. Things are grim.

 Inexperienced does not mean inadequate

Yesterday's indecency is today's mainstream. New categories of degeneracy crop up monthly—boundless sexuality, unchecked appetites, substance abuse, mutilation, violence, and death. Evil stalks in daylight, and our kids are exposed. Chap Clark captures the devastation well in his sobering book *Hurt*. Listen to the pain pouring through the words of this high school girl:

> *I was two when my dad walked out on me and my mom. My mom remarried the summer after fifth grade. I hated him. In sixth grade I lost my virginity. I just wanted to be loved by a guy. I hated my life, but when I had sex I felt like I was cared about and loved. I slept with three guys. Then in seventh I started to do drugs and drink. I would go to parties and stay out late. My mom kicked my stepdad out, so I was happy. School started. I was smoking and drinking a little here and there. I didn't really feel*

*loved or cared about. I felt dead inside. I picked up cutting. When
I saw myself bleed, I just felt so alive. To feel the pain was the best
feeling I could feel. My mom found out, so I stopped because I
had to see a counselor. A few months later I stopped eating. I had
to be perfect. I was the worst daughter. I had bad grades. I had a
bad attitude. My dad wasn't around. I felt like I was worthless. I
wasn't good enough for him. I feel like my life is worthless. I just
want to die half the time. I want to feel like I'm worth something,
loved, and cared for. Where do I find that?* [9]

Sometimes I'm shocked. More than once I've wandered the
trails near our house begging God for these kids. The pressures
they feel and temptations they face make my own seem trivial.
How can they possibly make it through unscathed?

The weight of it all used to make me feel helpless. How can I
solve their problems? How can I get them to want what's right in
the face of such momentum? How can I make them see down the
road, beyond the allure? Have you ever had these feelings? Do you
sometimes feel you're in over your head? That's a big temptation
when facing kid crises. It's easy to view yourself as inexperienced,
inadequate, and no match for the deviance you face.

Don't believe it.

If you can listen, love, and pray, you can make a difference.

Take the case of Susie, a middle-aged volunteer whose own
children were both in college. As she led a small group of juniors
she grew increasingly concerned about a girl named Andrea.
Though very pretty, Andrea appeared to be getting thinner by
the month.

After a group sleepover at Susie's house, it became obvious
there was a problem. Andrea picked at her dinner and passed on
breakfast.

Later that week, during a one-on-one hangout, Andrea confided that she viewed herself as fat. Susie listened carefully, praying all the while. A few clues emerged, prompting careful questions here and there. By the end of their conversation, Susie sensed that Andrea's self-perception was rooted in how she and her father related. She was very selective in which of her father's comments she remembered, and seemed bent on proving him wrong.

Andrea walked away from their one-on-one feeling heard and loved. Susie walked away with a better grip on how to pray and intercede for Andrea. That combination of listening, loving, and praying, made a big difference in Andrea's life. And in Susie's. (Having said that, if a student needs professional or medical help, take whatever steps are necessary.)

74 Get training when you can, but don't wait for it

Is psychological training helpful? Certainly. Would it be smart to read books about adolescents and communication skills? Absolutely. Will there be situations requiring professional intervention? Perhaps. But 95 percent of a youthworker's role is still *listening*, *loving*, and *praying*.

I once had breakfast with Dr. Larry Crabb, the well-known psychologist and author. Within fifteen minutes of sitting down together he described with startling accuracy all three of my primary relationships: father, mother, and wife. I was in awe, and listened carefully to everything he said after that. Would his level of skill come in handy when working with youth? Are you kidding? Sign him up! But are such skills necessary to effectively shepherd young people? Not at all. You'll do fine with what you have, starting today.

Still, I add to my skills inventory every chance I get. Read books. Go to seminars. Listen to CDs in your car. Download MP3 files from the Internet. There's so much helpful material within easy reach you don't need more school to gain a practical education. Get your associates to experience the same books, CDs, DVDs, and seminars as you do because in talking through what you learn, you'll learn it better.

Then as you begin to practice what you learn you'll have the joy of using newly acquired skills almost immediately. What a blast!

75 Focus on the heart, not the behavior

One of the girls in our group, Trisha, is dating the wrong guy. All he wants is personal gratification, and he's clever enough to keep her on the hook. Not that she makes it hard. A child of divorce, her need for male affection is considerable.

When Trisha's group leader first came to me about Trisha, she was visibly upset. Trisha had spent an hour, after group was over, crying and lamenting her mom's angry reaction to this boyfriend. Hard words were exchanged and threats were made, so Trisha was feeling torn between what felt like a right relationship and the distress of her mom.

Several weeks later I asked Trisha's group leader how things were going. "It seems better," she told me. "She hasn't broken up with him, but she didn't cry at all, and she seemed her normal self."

A month passed before I asked about Trisha again. "Well, she hasn't been to group this month because she's grounded. But I did talk to her at church . . . and she seemed different. She was hardened. When I asked how she was doing with her mom she said her mom was 'a case' and changed the subject."

Trisha is changing from tender to tough. She still has the boyfriend and remains estranged from her mom . . . who has responded with more groundings, restrictions, and consequences.

And I can list a dozen other families going through the same thing.

While it's true that Trisha is getting into deep water—unchecked deviance—it's not for lack of restraint. It's for lack of expressed love. We were created for love, not law, and love is the only thing that can reach a heart. Boundaries are important, and respecting authority is a biblical mandate. But if your goal is to reverse the tide of deviance, focus on the heart, not the behavior.

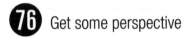 Get some perspective

We're all deviant. The things we can't have are the things we want. Any honest youthworker will admit to struggling with the same temptations as the average student. Sometimes those temptations are aroused just listening to the tales a student will tell. What makes an adult any better than a student if both struggle with the same things?

Perspective. We know better. We've failed, we've wrestled, and we've found our rest in Christ. We understand that "sin crouches at the door," lurking in the shadows, biding its time. Therefore, we cling to the grace of God and walk in daily dependence on Him. God is more important to us than our daily breath because we know we can't live without Him.

That's what makes your life worthy of imitation. You've learned it's not about willpower, but Christ's power. Deviance is no match for dependence.

77 Don't put yourself in compromising situations

During my early days of volunteering with our students, my "day job" was managing a gas station convenience store. We had a constant flow of employees moving through the store, including a young girl with considerable needs.

One day she came back to my office—which doubled as the access hallway to all the beverage coolers—and asked to talk with me. I yanked my backpack off the only other chair in the office and rolled my desk chair up close so I could hear her talk. We were probably not more than eight inches apart, with me leaning forward to catch her words, when the beer delivery guy walked in. He took one quick look at us, blurted out, "Whoa! Sorry Don!" and backed out again. The girl turned red, and my life, marriage, and ministry passed before my eyes.

My point? Never put yourself in a situation that could compromise your integrity, marriage, or ministry. Never. Think smart, like you're in a war and the enemy is out to get you. Be mindful of the danger zones. For example, I avoid situations that look bad (like sitting alone in a room close to someone of the opposite gender), connections that crackle with energy (ask, *Why do I want to meet with this person so strongly?*), and outright attraction (never alone, never deeply personal, and have someone else be the primary contact).

Although the Bible tells us, "Like a fluttering sparrow or a darting swallow, an undeserved curse does not come to rest" (Proverbs 26:2), it's better to blaze trouble-free trails. Establish prudent habits early on and you'll save yourself a world of regret.

78 Everyone wants security and significance

There are plenty of books explaining the way things are. I won't go into it here, except to say our culture is adrift (relativism) whereas our faith is fixed (on the character of God). As culture drifts further and further from the fixed point of God, the church drifts with it. After all, we live in the culture, not in a vacuum. Though we still use words and categories reflecting our fixed point, their meaning grows abstract with distance.

This tension is even more pronounced for kids than adults because their pace of drift is greater. Consider the following:

- Most of the modes of influence in youth culture circumvent parental control. The Internet is pervasive. The elegant iPod delivers its influence silently though sophisticated earpieces. Cell phones bypass household caller ID. Online social networks, text messaging, and email exist largely beyond the realm of parental awareness. Parents must work very hard to stay involved.

- The traditional mentoring role of parents has been assumed by teachers, coaches, peers, pastors, youthworkers, and . . . well, nobody. Who has time?

- Entertainment is more personal and more infused with its own morality than a generation ago. More kids are at the movies, on the Internet, or using electronic gaming devices than ever before. All these entertainment options feature a morality. Is it true, just, and righteous? Does it involve virtue, honor, and goodness?

The disparity is increasing between the character of God and the norms of today's adolescent community. Their resulting plunge into greater forms of deviance can catch us off guard and leave us feeling helpless. But don't be fooled. Though the symptoms and behaviors seem new, their root cause is as old as dirt. By refusing to overreact to the shocking, we can make large, stabilizing investments into their lives.

In Jeremiah 2:13, God speaks from the heart:

"My people have committed two sins:

> *They have forsaken me,*
> *the spring of living water,*

and have dug their own cisterns,
broken cisterns that cannot hold water."

Separation from God yields a frantic attempt to find *security* and *significance* elsewhere. All of life boils down to these fundamental, spiritual pursuits. And there are so many counterfeit cisterns in our country that an entire lifetime is not long enough to exhaust them.

Our students, while experimenting with new forms, are still moving in an age-old direction. And their most pressing need is for adults to keep pace with them in their struggle to find spiritual reality. To review Richard Dunn's remarks from an earlier chapter:

> Pacing requires me to listen to the heart of an adolescent, seeing beyond words and behaviors. Pacing therefore demands time, the time it takes to go beyond the surface in a conversation or to enter the social turf of a student —a band concert, a dorm room. Pacing is costly. The payoff, however, far exceeds the cost. Choosing to listen or to engage personally an adolescent's world communicates, "Who you are matters to me. I care about what you think, how you feel, and why you make the choices you do." Pacing builds trust. Trust builds relationship. Relationship conceives spiritual life exchanges. Such exchanges are the sacred places where the Holy Spirit reaches through the life of a Christian spiritual caregiver to change forever the life of a student.[10]

Take any category of struggle in your own life, whether with money, food, sexuality, or whatever. Chase the struggle far enough upstream and you'll find spiritual thirst. Learn to satisfy that thirst in God, let a young person see you doing it, and you will often see the student realign alongside you.

We've discussed deviance, and we know culture is not static. It's a tide that perpetually draws us away from the fixed point of God. Must we merely watch the drift and treat the casualties?

Why would we do that? Whose side are we on, anyway? Whose kingdom is among us, against which the gates of hell are defenseless? Never stop reminding yourself of these things. Nobody has us tied to the tracks. Take stock of the situation with your young people and—thinking as broadly and boldly as you can—decide how you can turn the course of culture back toward the fixed point of God and His created order.

Here's a small example of something we're getting proactive with. It's just one example out of many possibilities, but it's something we noticed and decided was important.

If you've been around for more than thirty years you know the dating scene has changed. It's become an endangered species. Why? The normal cycle of excess and overcorrection, probably. Dating mutated from getting to know a girl and her family in preparation for a lifelong commitment . . . to a recreational sport. And I don't mean wholesome recreation.

Then came a wave of corrective books to slow down (or even stop) the dating train. Their premise sounded something like this: *The social institution of dating has been given a fair trial and has failed miserably. It's time to abandon it for a better model.*

There's truth to this. As America transitioned from rural to urban and suburban, a new youth culture emerged. With increased discretionary time and money, young people began spending more unstructured time together, and dating evolved as an intermediate, special relationship between singleness and marriage. Meanwhile, the age of puberty dropped while the age of marriage increased, thereby increasing the spread of years during which young people had to remain pure. Throw in a permissive culture and a sexual revolution and what do you get? A mess.

But, consider the following . . .

I recently returned from this year's Dawntreader sailing trip. It was our twentieth such trip, and we took one hundred and fifty students. Now, if you're over the age of thirty-five, imagine being on this trip when you were in high school. Nearly twenty sailboats, each housing roughly four guys, four girls, and two adults. You're sailing through the enchanted waters of Canada's North Channel —fiords, cliffs, canyons, islands, and sunshine. Each night the boats anchor together in some private, magnificent cove and you run a fun-filled-but-deeply-spiritual program.

Here's my question: *When the trip was over, how many couples would you have?* More than you could count, right? Guess how many we had this year?

Zero.

At least in our area of the country, we've focused on the *problems* of dating for so long we've neglected to consider the alternatives. So now that the dating train is grinding to a halt and smoke is coming off the rails, how are young people getting to know one another in preparation for lifelong commitment? They're not. And they're not that interested in lifelong commitment, either.

When kids used to date, their parents would worry, right? They would also pray like crazy and provide rousing lectures about the dangers of premature intimacy. There was an attending decency to these concerns because they reflect the character of God and what He has in store for those who honor Him.

So what's happening? Are our kids suddenly chaste? Not at all. They're simply not bothering with relationship or commitment. Or love. Experimentation is in, commitment is out. And the future is at stake. We're like a town that shut down the coal plant because of its pollution, but now it's late afternoon, darkness is coming, the power is off, and we have no plans.

By praying a ton and studying what the Bible says about male-female relationships, our group has come up with a number of key principles for each gender. We're also training our young people to relate to one another in ways that reflect the character of God and His design for men and women.

Does this mean a return to dating at our church? I wouldn't put it that way. Rather, it means a return to guys doing what guys were created to do (move, lead, etc.), and girls responding in a way that reflects deep trust in God. Even though the fall of humanity wrought havoc on male-female relationships (see Genesis 3), we're created as new creatures in Christ, and there's a powerful rush involved in living out one's gender calling. It sets things back in their proper order so we can spend our time inspiring and equipping young people to strengthen one another rather than pouring countless hours into the assessment and healing of indescribable soul-damage.

The Old Testament makes a big deal about *justice*. It's emphasized repeatedly from Genesis to Malachi. A friend once described justice not as punishing bad behavior but as erecting fences along cliffs so people don't fall. When it comes to deviance, there are several points of focus for youthworkers. Listening. Loving. Praying. And setting up fences. Because there's always another class of students moving up through the ranks, and you can play a key role in keeping them from falling. ●

involve **parents**

OH, *how my eyes were opened at our first-ever "parents meeting." We had six kids in the group and I wanted to take them sailing. The meeting was scheduled to begin right after church, and I figured thirty minutes, max. Ten minutes of talk time, twenty for questions, then home for lunch by one o'clock.*

How green I was.

You're planning to do **what**? Do you have any idea how many people die in Lake Michigan every year? The bottom of that lake is littered with shipwrecks from one end to the other! Freighters travel those waters so fast you can't get out of their way! What makes you think I would let my daughter spend two weeks gallivanting across the North Channel in a boat full of boys? What are you trying to pull anyway? Our kids need to learn about God, not waste their summer being entertained like the world at the church's expense!

Everything I said provoked ten more questions. Nothing I said would calm their fears or quiet their suspicions. Perhaps I should have launched our program more modestly—say, with a nice quiet weenie roast behind the church on a Sunday afternoon . . .

Looking back, those parents had a point. I was attempting to put six landlubber kids aboard a thirty-seven-foot sloop-rigged sailboat and run them nonstop from Muskegon, Michigan, to Canada's great North Channel in Lake Huron. People from our area know the dangers of Great Lake wave patterns, especially in early June —the date I'd picked for our trip—when the water is still arctic and storms are routine.

Miraculously, we were able to run that first trip after all and—thank the Lord—it went well. Very well.

Perhaps that's why I didn't need to do any talking at all by my fourth parents' meeting. I simply thanked everyone for coming and turned the meeting over to Bob. Bob was forty-five years old, a business owner with a high school junior in the youth group, and highly respected in our community. He had also captained a boat for me the previous year.

Bob's presentation was straightforward. He walked to the front of the room, smiled at the other parents, and shared his experience. The more he talked about exposing our kids to God's creation via the breathtaking canyons and fiords of the Great North Channel, the more difficulty he had speaking. With tear-filled eyes he spoke of the soft-ness of kids' hearts and the love that bonded them together as they served one another onboard the boats. Those parents hung on his every word, and by the time he was done there wasn't a soul in the room who wouldn't have paid a thousand dollars to get his or her child on that trip.

At the time of this writing we just ran our twentieth sailing trip with nearly one hundred fifty students and thirty parents. How did we get here? We got here through the momentum and support of parent advocates. *When parents own the youth program, watch out!*

Parents are God's gift to young people and *youthworkers. They are the rightful and responsible guardians, nurturers, disciplers, and over-seers of our students. In everything we do, we are partnering with parents to "proclaim him, admonishing and teaching everyone with all wisdom, so that we may present everyone perfect in Christ" (Co-lossians 1:28). Involve parents in your ministry to their children and experience God's blessing and joy in your work. Not that it will always be easy. But it will be good.*

They're the good guys

I was twenty-seven-years old and he was forty-four. He had a troubled teenage son while I had a three-year-old who threw Cheerios from her highchair. I knew the dreaded, four-letter words were coming long before he opened his mouth. *Just wait!* he warned in that classic, condescending voice of a parent in pain. *You'll understand what I mean in a few years.*

How does a young youthworker stand a chance in conversations with parents of teenagers? How does one communicate support and assistance when viewed as a rookie?

Without careful consideration, such a situation can degenerate into a mutually threatening stalemate. The parent is threatened because his or her student thinks the youthworker walks on water. The youthworker is threatened because the parent assumes insight is limited to age and experience. This is lose-lose territory. Don't go there. Instead learn to do these things:

- Encourage them
- Pray for them
- Partner with them

Parents are your greatest allies.

 Listen to them

Our culture does not value listening. At best we wait people out while inwardly thinking our own thoughts. Yet to truly listen to another person is to communicate love—and love is a principle ingredient when working with parents. To get a feel for how this works, consider the following two statements that are generally true of most parents:

- Parents know their children better than anyone else.
- Parents love their children more than anyone else.

I make these two observations to most parents I meet with. And as I mention them, most parents visibly relax on the spot. To acknowledge these truths is one of the most calming gifts you can offer an overly anxious mom or dad.

Of course, if you truly believe these things to be true, put your money where your mouth is. Try not to do more than 10 percent of the talking, and listen with all your heart. Listen to their words, through their words, around their words, and behind their words. And pray as you listen. Ask God to reveal what you should hear through all this listening.

When it comes time to speak, use the same listening techniques I mentioned in chapter 4 (*Learn how to listen and then actually listen. . .*).

Listening well wins the heart of the person who is heard. It is a powerful form of love, and one largely overlooked. When I ask a question, I am actually honoring a parent by implying I trust her perceptions and instincts. This, in turn, gives her the freedom to drop her defenses, process the situation being discussed, and come to terms with what is happening.

Granted, things won't always come off as easily as I'm suggesting (which we'll discuss in a moment), but learning to listen in love provides an excellent baseline for working with parents.

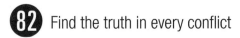 **82** Find the truth in every conflict

In most conflict there is a kernel of truth. Finding it amidst all the criticism and defensiveness is the problem.

Becoming defensive comes as naturally as breathing. That's why it takes training to respond constructively. And believe me, a small investment here can provide a tenfold return in maintaining healthy relationships with parents.

What I often say to a parent who is critical of our program (or of me personally) is:

> "I appreciate you sharing your concern with me. At this point I need some think time. I'll commit to praying about this for a few days to see how God would like to use your input in my life. Let me get back with you in a week or so, okay?"

Such a response accomplishes several things. First, you let them know their concern has been heard. Second, you demonstrate an openness to grow and show that you value God's work in your life. Third, you let them know you'll take it to heart by following up on it. Finally, you give yourself time to consider what's been said without the tension and defensiveness that clouded the initial conversation.

To seek first to understand rather than to be understood is not basic human instinct. But if God has set you apart to work with students, your calling comes with the colorful blessing of also working with parents. And, believe me, I know working with parents can be extremely colorful because . . . I am one.

One time, back when my son was in seventh grade, I took him and his friend to a new small group led by one of our high school students. When I picked them up three hours later they were exploding with energy. "It was totally cool, Dad! Max took us to Burger King in his new truck!"

Instantly, my parental instincts kicked into high gear. You see, I knew Max, and I knew about his truck. It was a small truck with a single seat up front. I also knew there were at least nine kids at his house that night. The truth is, I know a lot of stuff because I'm old. I know that nine junior high boys in the back of a tiny pickup for ten miles at sixty-plus miles per hour is not a good thing. I know that a first-year driver soaring on adrenaline is not a good thing. And I know every boy in that group will go home and regale his parents with fast-paced tales of their outrageous adventure. I know too much.

Now consider everything I know and all the emotion I'm feeling at that moment. Then imagine my conversation with Max. The poor kid.

Was there a kernel of truth in my concern? You bet there was! Did I offer more than a kernel of truth? Right again! More like a couple dump trucks full. And was I in a better frame of mind a week later? Yes. I was.

 ## The twenty-four-hour rule

The volleyball coach from our large high school said it well when speaking to a group of charged-up parents. "Don't talk to me after a game about how much time your daughter got to play. Give yourself twenty-four hours and then call me."

Emotions are a strange deal. They come and they go. They can be lighter than air or heavier than cement. Sometimes intoxicating, at other times devastating. Yet there is one thing entirely consistent about them. They are *not* trustworthy.

At our church, we abide by a twenty-four-hour rule, which goes like this—you get twenty-four hours after being attacked to let your emotions expend themselves. But after that, you must take up a towel and wash feet.

Why does this help? Because it acknowledges the reality of emotions while not allowing them to drive behavior.

If a nasty letter crosses my desk, I don't even fight it. I know I'll get defensive. I know I will scheme, manipulate, fight, shift blame, and so on. I also know that within twenty-four hours I will move toward that person with a redemptive plan. And that's what brings the kingdom of God into the brotherhood of believers. Is there any greater privilege than that?

84 Six habits to practice with parents

I felt bad for him. Real bad. Though he was experienced in youth-work, he was new at the church. And his new church had a history of suspicion toward its youth pastors.

That's probably why he started six months early. He called the first meeting in mid-January, and followed it up with church-wide marketing and student-leader recruitment. It was shaping up to be the best trip his youth group had ever experienced.

But then one of the parents stood up at a board meeting in late May and put the brakes on. Why did he do it? Was he fearful for his daughter? Was he threatened by the potential success of my friend? Was he offended at some comment, rumor, facial expression, or poster in my friend's office? Who knows? Nevertheless, he got the trip cancelled and halted the early momentum of my friend's new youth program.

This begs a huge question. *How do we get parents to own a vision for students and their spiritual formation?*

I believe we do it through prayer. In his book *Deepening Your Conversation with God*, Ben Patterson remarks that *prayer is the work and ministry is the fruit*. I believe he's right, and so I lay a foundation of prayer for everything I do.

I also practice six regular habits with our parents:

- **Clarity**—As leaders, we must be crystal clear when explaining what we're trying to accomplish. As I've already confided, this requires much prayer. It also involves think time and refinement. Before you present an idea it should be crisp, concise, and powerful.

- **Exposure**—I love exposing parents to spiritual growth in students. Whether on a trip or in the relationally charged discussions of a small group, parents need to see what's happening in the hearts of their students and catch the fever themselves.

- **Vision**—It takes vision to stir up a parent base. The conviction you show will be contagious—first with a select few, and then throughout the group. This is a crucial point of recruiting and sharing the ministry.

- **Experience**—After they've heard and caught the vision, arrange for parents to run some aspect of the program.

- **Ownership**—Once parents get a taste of participating with the Spirit of God in the spiritual transformation of students, there will be no problem with ownership. In fact, other problems will come to the forefront. Have I mentioned the time we had more parents signed up for a mission trip than students? That was a delicate affair . . .

- **Advocacy**—I've already commented on the difference between my first parent meeting and my fourth (see the introduction to this chapter). The bottom line from that experience is this—once parents have ownership of a trip or program, you'll almost never have to promote or defend it. Parents have a wonderful way of networking together and championing things they believe in.

85 Go the extra mile to keep parents in the loop

Communicating with parents is a strange science. We recently devoted an entire meeting to the relative merits of websites, email, handouts, bulletins announcements, phone message chains, and postcards. It would be easier if we could adopt a standard format and have it work, but the truth is, nothing really works. Consequently, we need to use every technique at our disposal to keep as many of the parents informed as possible.

An informed parent is a wonderful thing to behold. All grace, peace, and confidence. Conversely, a parent who senses the world (and her child) passing her by will be perpetually agitated.

I love to observe the difference in parent meetings that feature handouts contrasted with those that have none. Parents love to know things. I know I do. My three kids went through our program and even I wanted to know where they were staying and what the adult-to-student ratio would be on every trip. I wanted to know how to pray and what the red flags were. The more I knew, the better.

This is so basic I think it's impossible to overcommunicate.

Several years ago we dreamed a dream. We got this awesome website up and running and made it the greatest thing in the known world. And it worked. Sort of. Twenty-five percent of our students and parents used it. We assumed it would take the congregation by storm and revolutionize communication standards in our entire region. Right.

The reality is: the website has it, the bulletin has it, the email says it, the postcard says it, and the parent meeting handouts explained it. And some parents are still going to call the night before the trip demanding to know why they were never told.

I once kept track of my phone calls the day before a big trip. I had 156 of them. (I should have recorded the information on my voicemail message instead of answering the phone!)

We all roll our eyes when the question at hand has already been answered dozens of times, but the key isn't really in providing information. It's in graciously and lovingly explaining it again as if for the very first time. Because *an honored, informed, involved, and praying parent is the best thing that can ever happen to your youth program.* ●

develop **strong** leaders

SAILING *looks glamorous. Strike a pose at the helm and you're Captain Adventure. But add some real wind or rough seas and all you can think about is* I sure could use some help up here!

One year we added a new captain to our sailing trip. He'd been sailing Lake Michigan for decades and knew every nuance of weather, water, shoals, and coves. What he didn't know was the meaning of crew.

I'll never forget watching him leave the marina. The breeze was stiff and this guy was charging about the deck as though on fire. Hoisting this, tightening that, and always checking the charts. He was a cyclone of commotion. And surrounding him in the cockpit were eight able-bodied high school students keeping out of his way.

We'd set an ambitious goal that day—seven hours of tricky sailing with a shallow cove at the end. I knew he'd make it, but I knew something else too. He would either discover the wonders of teamwork, or he'd be toast.

As it turned out, he learned quickly. By the end of the week he looked like all the other captains—casually perched near the stern, accomplishing more with a few words to his eight-member crew than ever would have been possible by rushing about.

Shared leadership is a lifesaver, whether you're working with six young people or six hundred. Share the privilege by involving as many others as God places within reach. The apostle Paul reveals this as a key ingredient of spiritual growth in Ephesians 4:11–16—many members working together for the benefit of all. I can't stress this enough. Whether you're a paid youthworker or an occasional volunteer, look for ways to share the process. Discipleship is a team exercise.

---

86 Decide what type of leader you'll be

The best way to understand leadership is to recall the leaders you've served under. It's easier to weigh the pros and cons of different leadership styles when you're the one withering under a poor leader or feeling empowered by a good one.

The extremes are amazing. Have you ever served under someone who kept control over all that mattered? I know a woman who was scolded for tidying a supply closet at a daycare center. Apparently her college degree didn't qualify her to organize crayons and scissors.

Why cling to the reins so tightly? I'm not sure. Perfectionism? A fear of mistakes? Or maybe a fear of things not being done "just the way you want them." But it could also reveal insecurity. Some leaders are threatened by the success of subordinates. Remember Israel's King Saul when David was slaying his ten thousands? Yikes.

In contrast, consider the leader who is secure in her relationship with Christ and lives to see Him work in young people's lives. Such a leader recognizes the giftedness of others and thrives on empowering them to develop their gifts. Healthy leaders see the larger picture and realize we are not rewarded for what we accomplish, but what we become—and help others to become—in the process.

In his book *Good to Great*, Jim Collins makes a startling observation about truly great leaders. After sifting through research into hundreds of companies, he and his team discovered the great leaders—the ones who achieved unparalleled success—had one thing in common. *Humility.*

This isn't to say only humble leaders are successful. A great many gifted people achieve profound success. But the leaders who achieve long-term results don't see themselves as the solution to every problem. They empower others to share in meeting the challenge.

Whether you are a volunteer or a paid youthworker, be a servant-leader. Empower others to discover and exercise their God-given abilities. Then make it your goal to fan such abilities into flame.

87 Learn the difference between chaperones and investors

You and I have both seen them. For some reason they sign up for trips and events, and even seem interested in young people. But they don't know how to do it. Instead of mixing with the students, they stand on the fringe talking with other adults. Sometimes they'll even make wry comments about student behavior. Yet they never invest in making things better. They don't get involved.

I think of these people as *chaperones.*

It takes a lot of adults to maintain a healthy level of investment in students. Thankfully, at least in most churches, there are plenty of adults to choose from. Each one occupies a different point on the path to Christlikeness, and all have unique gifts. So how should you choose leaders to help with students?

I start by distinguishing between *investors* and *chaperones.* Some adults will be chaperones forever. They're intimidated by students, or critical of them. It's always *us* and *them.* But others can never forget what it was like to be young. In fact, some of the best youth-workers seem locked into that stage of life. They still see themselves as insecure freshmen, holding a tray of food and looking for a place to sit in an unfriendly cafeteria. These people naturally gravitate to students. They can't help it.

And students can't get enough of it. It's true, you know. Ask kids what they really want and, once you penetrate the surface of fun and entertainment, most will say *someone to listen and care.* These are your *investors.*

88 Don't just plug warm bodies in empty slots

My mistake was to lock this guy into a normal area of ministry. Because I enjoyed his friendship I naturally assumed he would enjoy the same things I did.

Right.

It wasn't until years later I realized what a driven person he was. A high achiever whose pace of life was unbelievable. Had I thought about it, I could have orchestrated a rich experience for him to use his gifts. He would have thrived on temporary assignments involving adventure and problem solving. What he didn't thrive on was teaching junior high Sunday school for fifty-two weeks every year.

Put four adults in a room full of high school students and two will get all revved up. They won't be able to remember the last time they felt so alive. The other two will call in sick next time. But ask them to drive a bus or host an event and they'll get up at four in the morning to be ready in time.

One of the best ways to place volunteers is to expose them to a wide variety of roles and responsibilities. I often have people approach me because they want to be "involved with youth." Most of them have no clue what that looks like. When asked direct questions about their interests they present a blank stare.

What I usually do at that point is have them get their feet wet in different areas. I'll ask them to go on a retreat, substitute teach, help organize a trip, visit a small group, and maybe take a student to lunch. This helps them discover their *motivated abilities.*

Don't look for warm bodies to fill slots. Match slots with gifting. Don't assume because someone can teach he should take the next class that comes open. Maybe he *can* teach, but he *thrives* on mentoring. Short, temporary assignments bring giftedness and motivation into focus. Match volunteers with their sweet spots and you'll have long-term partners.

All of us are good at certain things. Conversely, we all have responsibilities that drain our energy and rob our joy. Imagine the electricity of helping leaders discover roles that energize them! No joke—it's one of those things that makes you feel like you're partnering with God. Because you are.

89 Remember we're on the same side

After ten days of equatorial heat, no showers, and Montezuma's Revenge, nobody wanted to waste time getting home. So we drove nonstop, as usual, with me taking the last leg of a red-eye run. Thanks to the modern miracle of cell phones we arrived home to a parking lot swarming with moms, dads, siblings, aunts, uncles, cousins, and minivans. Arriving home from a trip is always a celebration and I usually love it. But this time the first person I saw when the bus door swung open blurted out, "Hey Don! How was your vacation?"

Let's be honest. Few people know what a full-time youthworker does for a living. *Wears T-shirts to work, eats with students, performs funny skits on Sunday, and travels to exotic places. Not to be confused with a real job.* So when a business guy who's working killer hours and getting up at four in the morning to catch some "no meeting time" in the office sees a tanned dude in sandals exiting a bus with sixty happy teenagers, he's thinking: *That's the life.*

Meanwhile, the tanned dude is returning from his third consecutive trip. He's only spent three days with his family during the past month, and now he's facing several eighty-hour weeks of meetings, discipleship sessions, teaching classes, finding volunteers for the fall session, running small groups at night, and preparing for the Sunday sermon later this month. Plus two weddings and a twice-postponed graduation party. He'll be lucky to catch two evenings at home any week before Labor Day, and at some point before snow flies he should replace the bald tires on his '87 Honda Accord. At the moment he's got the runs so bad he'd better sprint to the church before humiliation strikes . . . except there's this affluent business guy who drives a Lexus and plays golf on Sundays standing in his way accusing him of living on the dole.

Now picture what happens several days later when the tanned dude asks the stressed-to-the-max business guy to lead a Bible study for sophomore boys. What's the biz guy thinking? He's thinking, *Hey, isn't that what we pay you for? I work for a living and can barely hang on, while all you do is think of more ways to entertain these kids. Where do you get off thinking I've even got two minutes to call my own let alone do your job for you! If you don't have time to lead a Bible study, maybe you should cancel some of those game nights or trips to Six Flags!*

And what's the tanned dude thinking? *Here I am sacrificing my life, my marriage, my family, and my health trying to keep your kids in relationship with God, and you won't even bother lifting a finger! I'm exhausted to the bone, have zero money in the bank and no retirement fund, can't take my wife anyplace special for our tenth anniversary, and can't possibly cram enough hours of study into my week to teach Sunday school, preach a sermon, lead two Bible studies, and do a lunchtime devotional at the local high school. And you won't even help me out of a pinch!*

This is no joke. These are real conflicts that few people actually flesh out.

People leave churches over this stuff, and youthworkers burn out (or worse) because of it. So be alert . . . remain steadfast in prayer . . . and remember "Our struggle is not against flesh and blood, but against the rulers, against the authorities, against the powers of this dark world and against the spiritual forces of evil in the heavenly realms" (Ephesians 6:12). This calls for lots of grace.

90 Say "Thank You"

Whether working with students is a paid youthworker's job or the job of parents and church members, here's something that's simply good practice *and* good manners. Say thank you! If someone helps out and you know about it, thank her. Even better, thank her *and ask how it went.*

Be creative with this. Do it in person with eye contact and smiling. Use the phone. Send emails. If someone helps a lot or needs special affirmation—all the better. Think of some surprising or creative way to deliver your gratitude. For example:

- Create an invoice, detailing the work you received from the person. List their hours and pay rate (make it honorably substantial) and total it at the bottom. Then sign it off as a gift or stamp it as paid in full. This lets them know you understand the value of their time.

- Leave a voicemail for the entire family so they can listen to your gratitude.

- Text a simple message with words truncated on purpose.

- Snail mail is so old it's cool. Send a card or letter . . . in your own handwriting!

- Gift certificates for coffee are a caffeine hit for the soul.

Nothing lifts the spirits like knowing your involvement was appreciated, and most people would rather feel part of something than fly solo. Your interest in how it went, and your sacrifice of time to discuss it for a few minutes can make the difference be-tween one-shot helpers and long-term partners.

Regardless of how busy you feel, place a high priority on gratitude.

91 Establish parity between staff and volunteer time

It didn't take long at the outset of our youth program to spot the tension between full-time and volunteer youthworkers. All it takes is a little growth and the tempers flare. So, after much prayer and wise counsel, we decided to establish parity between the two. In our case we learned that the average parent or volunteer was put-ting in roughly sixty hours per week between work and church. (By "church" I mean all the time a person spends either sitting or serving in church.)

So that became our standard. After all, there's no reason paid workers should be investing any less than those we're hired to serve. Nor is there reason to abandon family, faith, or health by overdoing it. The Master is capable of recruiting laborers for His harvest. We pray for them every day (Matthew 9:38).

Few things have strengthened the level of respect between our paid and volunteer workers than the common understand-ing that we're all serving sacrificially in this grand endeavor. Two quick stories come to mind:

First, I remember a certain board meeting where one of the men—a hard-working businessman—commented on how encour-aged he was to see the pastor's car in the parking lot at 6:00 a.m. every morning as he passed on his way to work. He actually felt like the souls of our people were in good hands (Hebrews 13:17).

Second, I remember watching a couple of volunteers on the other side of a campfire one night. There they were investing in our students long after dark . . . even though it was a rough time for their business and they were putting in upwards of eighty hours a week trying to keep it afloat. I actually sat there that night praying for *them*.

92 Encourage student leadership

Is anything more exciting than watching a student catch fire for Jesus and model His life among family, friends, and peers at school?

I was talking with a senior the other day at his soccer game. I had been confused earlier in the week because I saw his name on two student leader lists. But when I asked for clarification my confusion switched to amazement. Not only was he leading both groups at church—he had also formed two groups at school. He was literally leading four student groups every week!

Student leaders have advantages those of us with jobs, spouses, kids of our own, and decades of life experience no longer have. Time, energy, and unbridled optimism.

There's no way I could pull off everything he was achieving, but I could do something just as important. I could come alongside him and set him up for success. That boy was on fire for Jesus, and he was clearly working within his area of gifting. But it takes more than gifting and energy to succeed. It takes encouragement, direction, big-picture vision, words of caution, and lots of prayer. In short, it takes involvement.

Student leadership is essential to youth ministry. But as you encourage and develop student leaders, remember to match gifting with tasks. Consider the following opportunities for ministry and the various abilities required. Some are bite-sized while others require extensive gift-development:

- Student spotlight—sharing a five minute insight into what God is doing in your life

- Planning a two-hundred mile route for a backcountry bike trip

- Organizing a worship band for a retreat

- Developing a PowerPoint presentation for a fund-raising event

- Taking another student out for a one-on-one challenge

- Writing a Bible study that will be one of five used on the Mexico trip

- Setting up chairs for the weekly program

- Developing a skit

- Creating a sports league for outreach

- Praying for younger students (by name) as their retreat approaches

We are in the business of developing students for lifetimes of loving and serving God. This involves letting them participate as both servants and leaders. It also requires risk-taking, exposure, coaching, patience, and follow-through. But the rewards far exceed what you will experience if adults do all the leading and students have no opportunity to follow their Lord or exercise their gifts.

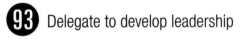 **Delegate to develop leadership**

It dawned on me after he left my office just what had happened. While meeting with an intern I added three things to my "to do" list. He added nothing to his.

Whoops.

Delegation requires diligence. Even if it doesn't come naturally to you, keep trying, because your effectiveness as a leader depends on it. And there's a lot more to delegation than telling others what to do. For a student leader, it might look like giving a book to a friend. An adult volunteer might "delegate" responsibility by finding a prayer partner for her group. And a paid youthworker might hand responsibility for a major initiative to someone with more time, resources, or . . . gifting.

For all of us, it must be viewed as part of the empowering process whereby others can develop their gifts.

The tricky part of delegating is making sure the receiving partner feels entrusted with something of value. Contrast the following two assignments:

- I'm extremely busy today. Could you swing by the cleaners and pick up my shirts? That would help me a ton.

- Our winter retreat is six months away. I was wondering what area you feel most qualified to oversee or help out with?

In both cases the person receiving an assignment will probably do the job, but the implications are obvious. One will leave feeling empowered and the other will feel like an errand boy. *The key to remember is that you are developing leaders, not accumulating servants.* Delegating is such an important part in the leadership development process because it allows different people to begin to learn different roles.

94 Assess honestly and affirm liberally

He had just run his first trip. I'd run it the previous thirteen years, but this year it was his and I'd come along only to observe. Right now we were sitting across coffee for the purpose of evaluation.

Can you see the look in his eye? Can you sense the tension in his silence? At some level he wants constructive feedback, but mostly he wants what? *Affirmation.*

I have more experience with trips than he does. We both know that. But the scope of our ministry will never expand if I don't delegate some trips to others. Besides, he's a talented young guy and the students like him. We both know that too.

How would you conduct such a meeting? It's of critical importance for you, him, and the ongoing effectiveness of your work. What should it sound like? Here are a few tips:

- **Be specific**—In as many categories as possible, I want to offer specific advice and give specific examples. For instance, "I noticed that in our big group sessions you had some awkward moments when you asked if anyone wanted to close in prayer. When no one volunteered it seemed like the tension grew. Here are a couple of options you may want to consider for next time: either ask someone ahead of time, or call on someone by name. Pick a person who is tracking with you and will add strength to what's going on. That way you'll inspire confidence rather than promote a general uneasiness."

- **Allow for stretching**—As a result of our evaluation meeting I want my understudy to catch the vision for an even better "next time." This involves dreaming together without me dictating the exact path such dreaming should follow. For instance, questions like these may find their way into our discussion:

  - *What could we do to make an even bigger bang during the last large group meeting? What's something they'd never forget?*

  - *I've noticed our worship times only engage about half of the students. How could we improve that?*

  - *How effective do you think the quiet time study booklets were? What was good about them and what weaknesses could be fixed for next time?*

In contrast to being specific in my critique, this category invites my new leader to dream with me. It humbly implies that I don't have all the answers and suggests that he can take what I developed and make it better. It communicates my confidence in him.

- **Convey trust**—If I want a leader to leave our meeting confident of my trust, three things should be communicated:

  1. The next time you run this trip, I'll be completely out of the picture.

  2. I'm eager to watch you improve this program.

  3. Think about the leaders you want to develop the next time you run this trip.

95 Watch your staffing ratios

Youthwork is a demanding, urgent, and taxing exercise. For example:

- **Critical stage of life**—Perhaps more than any other stage of life, adolescence demands focused attention. Big decisions are made and key life directions are chosen.

- **Independence**—If they are to survive as adults, young people must forge their own life and identity. However, even though this transition must occur, it can involve tremendous stretching and pain. Anyone in such a transitory phase needs help and support.

- **Parents**—The ones who are *most* desperate for assistance are actually the parents. If you have twenty-five "stretching" students in your program you'll have fifty (or more!) overwrought parents.

To help you weather the great demands of youthwork, healthy staffing ratios will play a key role. Here are two benchmarks we use:

- Volunteers-to-Students 1:5

- Paid Staff-to-Students 1:50

Admittedly, there are always adjustments to be made. A trip to Mexico will demand different ratios than a run to the amusement park. However, the above guidelines are a good starting point.

96 Know when to ask for help and when to pay for it

Let's say you and a few other volunteers are working together with ten students. Should you hire a full-time worker to help out? Probably not. But what if you're shepherding fifty students? At what point does opportunity outpace capacity? Keep your eye on that balance and prayerfully consider your situation. Here are a few issues to weigh during your discussions:

- Does it make sense to move a volunteer into a paid position? Consider what's best for the organization *and* the person. While hiring people certainly acknowledges their significant contributions, it can also rob them of the joys and rewards of volunteer service.

- Paying someone to *do* ministry and paying someone to *develop* ministry are not the same thing. Paying people to *do* in one area can create tension as those *doing* in other areas make comparisons. Consider what you want a full-timer doing (or *developing*) before bringing one on.

- Hiring part-timers can ease the transition from running a volunteer-based program to bringing on a full-time youthworker. However, it is often said that part-timers put things on your list while full-timers take things off your list.

Obviously, who you hire will determine whether this proves true or not, but it's important to keep in mind.

- Two- to five-year projections should come before hiring decisions. An intern at $1,200 may seem attractive when you're in a pinch, but make sure your pinch isn't signaling a systemic change. Conversely, don't commit to a full-timer if you're simply weathering a back-to-school surge. There's no easy way to project this perfectly, but many churches assess hours invested, as follows:

  - Interns log ten to twenty hours per week

  - Youth assistants invest twenty to thirty hours weekly

  - When your group consistently calls for over thirty hours, hire a full-timer

Also, be careful to work out specific responsibilities and compensation before talking with candidates. The only thing rougher than needing help is battling over unmet expectations and compensation grievances with a hastily hired youthworker.

97 Know how to recognize good college interns

If you live near a college town (as we do), you'll review plenty of internship applications (especially if you're near a Christian college). Most education or youthworker majors require an internship, and nearly all college students need money. So how can you spot those who will leave the indelible impression of God on the lives of your students? (Hint: it has nothing to do with tattoos or piercings.) Here are the factors we use to sort through candidates:

- **Agenda**—I meet college students all the time who love youthwork because it's more fun than being responsible.

If you suspect someone has an agenda other than helping students grow in Christ, give them a hard assignment and watch them avoid you from now on. (For example, assign a book to read and have them report back to you when finished.)

- **Money**—College students need money. That's a given. And you may have some in your budget. But is this the best way to spend it? Hiring interns should only come after you've decided how many dollars you'll invest in staffing rather than programming.

- **Discretionary time**—How much time do you have to invest in developing workers who will only be around for a year? There's not a *right* answer to this question—I've done it, and I know of several other organizations that make a habit of it. It's a great way to participate in God's work around the world. However, there may be right and wrong *times* to invest beyond your own group. If you're in a development or building phase, I recommend long-term investments on the home front.

- **Assimilation**—Can your program assimilate interns with its current rate of growth? In other words, will you be able to hire the interns you train? If yes, choose interns as though hiring long-term staff.

- **Short-timer relationships**—Am I helping my students if I hire an intern who will only be available for one year? Is this the best thing for students who will be with me for four years? How about interns who are willing to commit to two years? The equation is flexible; just make sure and ask up front.

Of course, I've tipped my hand a bit. We currently use between two and five interns at any given time. The things that matter most to us are long-term commitment to our church, humility, note-worthy impact with the students, and teachability.

98 Train your leaders

Think of all the specialists you wouldn't trust if they weren't trained: airline pilots, auto mechanics, dentists, surgeons, computer technicians, construction engineers, and so on. Make sure the people who shepherd your students are on that list as well. They may be busy, but that doesn't mean you can't equip them for service. We've used all of the following options over the past twelve months to train our workers:

- **Seven to seven**—This was an off-site event we ran from 7:00 a.m. till 7:00 p.m. one Sunday. We broke the day into formal training, free time, prayer walks, and small group kick-off planning. It worked really well and helped to forge a bond within our team.

- **Once a month**—We run one-hour training sessions every month for most of our leaders. It's fun to see a classroom filled with those who love young people. One night I stood in the back and noted a fifty-year age range between the participants—student leaders and seventy-year-olds were learning together how to serve others. You can offer these classes during the Sunday school hour if you want, and don't forget to "borrow" good ideas from anyone you know of who is working effectively with youth.

- **NYC**—The National Youth Workers Convention is always a treat and offers something for everyone. With worship, motivational speakers, and over one hundred elective seminars, NYC delivers momentum every time we use it.

- **Resources**—Be generous with books, CDs, and DVDs. We add to our training library practically every week. The great thing about resources is that they're contagious— direct someone to a new Podcast about running a trip or mentoring students and watch how fast that message spreads among your team. Nothing beats viral training.

- **Curriculum**—The longer you work with young people the more wisdom you glean from the experience. That's why we often write our own curriculum for groups and training. Every member of your team, whether paid or occasional, will benefit from what the team has learned. If you can keep everyone up to speed with the insights you've gleaned, you'll all have more time to invest in students rather than struggling through already-solved dilemmas.

 God's vision—share it

Leadership produces a curious tension. Get caught up in the visibility, authority, and recognition, and you'll soon hit a ceiling. But allow God to do His kingdom work through you and emerging leaders will continually spring up in your wake. This applies whether you're paid or volunteering.

I have a guy who works under me. On one occasion I shared a vision with him. "Hey Bob—what if we developed a student worship band under the direction of an adult volunteer?" He liked the idea, ran with it, and within a year had five rotating worship bands. Unbelievable. If I'd decided to hold on to that vision for myself it would still be nothing more than a few scrawled lines in the "Some Day" column of my daily planner.

Giving leadership away is a tricky business. If you're like me, you'll constantly be tempted to reach for the controls. On one occasion I stepped back into something I had delegated. Sensing frustration and political unrest, I thought to myself, *I'd better run that trip myself.* The problem was, it was no longer "my trip." He'd already run several of them, and they beautifully reflected his gifting and expertise. My oversight turned out to be a liability—it divided the new leadership he'd put in place, disrupted his planning, and postponed a good opportunity for him to learn the nuances of political wisdom.

On the plus side, I learned a valuable lesson. Shared leadership is not just about casting vision and delegating tasks. It also involves the twin disciplines of trust . . . and prayer. ●

one last thing

OF the one hundred and fifty members of my senior class, he was one of the leading pot smokers. By a wide margin.

He was also the biggest risk-taker in the entire school. Maybe even the state. At 165 pounds, he led the football conference in tackles, and during track and field season he kept using longer and longer poles, zealous to soar into those unsafe, atmospheric regions. More than once I watched him crash-land when a pole—too stiff for his weight—hurled him beyond the cushioned mat.

I can remember praying for him for years, going over my list at night. Others did too, backing up their prayers with lives that demonstrated the love of our God. Faithfulness without fanfare.

Finally, during his college years, he came face-to-face with the grace of God.

Now his risk-taking nature had a cause—and a Leader —worthy of all that outrageous drive and devotion. He followed with all his might.

As a missionary.

To Pakistan.

And later, Macedonia.

I recently spent time with him, catching up on the thirty years since graduation. We talked of marriage, kids, and the stuff of life. And through it all there was a fire in his eyes, occasionally softened by moisture, reflecting the fully stoked fire in his heart for the lost. Undeterred by years spent in unsafe regions, the urgency in his soul still drives him to press on. To take risks. In the service of the King.

Would you like to know who eventually led him to Christ? It was someone humble. Nondescript. A servant, in love with God and working with youth.

It was someone like you.●

sample characteristics of spiritual maturity

TO help prime your DDP pump, here are sample characteristics gleaned from what other churches have come up with. This list is in no way exhaustive, so use it as a starting point. And remember to draw from your own well (that way you'll have ownership too).

- Essential skills (prayer, evangelism, etc.)

- Essential relationships (God, family, etc.)

- Essential attitudes (humility, faith, etc.)

- Essential knowledge (deity of Christ, inerrancy of Scripture, etc.)

- Believes

- Worships

- Serves

- Evangelizes

- Gives

- Relates

- Healthy relationship to God

- Healthy relationship to self

- Healthy relationship to others

- Healthy relationship to creation

- Believes what the Bible says about God is true

- Walks in the Spirit

- Seeks the kingdom

- Lives in community

- Feeds on truth

- Demonstrates God

- Practices influence

- Builds redemptive relationships

- Defends the faith

- Links compassion with Gospel

- Capable of communicating the Gospel with own story and style

- Demonstrates love for God through obedience

- Engages God in worship (both corporately and individually)

- Demonstrates skills that enable worship

- Persistent in Bible reading and prayer

- Willingly leads in prayer

- Reflects the character of God

- Committed to a small group community

- Demonstrates a proper relationship to authority

- Evaluates his/her own style of relating

- Cultivates an accountability relationship

- Embraces tension between being "in" but not "of" the world

- Understands and uses spiritual gifts within the Church

- Willingly serves others

- Demonstrates a good work ethic

- Grateful giver

- Takes personal responsibility for his or her faith (development)

- Understands God's story

- Understands and applies Scripture

- Makes decisions from a biblical value set

- Understands a biblical view of man

NOTES

CHAPTER 3

1. Kevin Huggins is the author of *Parenting Adolescents* and *Friendship Counseling*. Though I don't recall the exact name or date of the conference I attended, Kevin's session helped me understand student needs from a biblical perspective.
2. Richard R. Dunn, *Shaping the Spiritual Life of Students* (Downers Grove: InterVarsity, 2001), 16.
3. The statement, "Emotions reveal the price tags of events and relationships," came from the same presentation by Kevin Huggins referenced in Note 1.
4. R. A. Torrey, *How to Pray* (Chicago: Moody, 2007), 119–120.

CHAPTER 4

5. In *Raising Self-Reliant Children in a Self-Indulgent World*, H. Stephen Glenn (along with coauthor Jane Nelson) emphasizes the lost art of dialogue. He frequently expanded upon this theme at conferences and seminars, like the National Youth Workers Convention I attended some time in the 1980's, long before I ever dreamed of writing a book. This definition is taken from the notes I took at that event.
6. Dietrich Bonhoeffer, Life Together (San Francisco: Harper & Row, 1954), 28.

CHAPTER 5

7. The phrase, "first, most, and always," is a song title (track 3) borrowed from the CD *Run*, by Strong Tower Band (STB1810-3).
8. The phrase, "living a life worthy of imitation," is the title of a lecture series on leadership by the late Dave Busby. At the time of this writing, a CD of this series can be purchased at: http://www.davebusby.com/

CHAPTER 8

9. Chap Clark, *Hurt* (Grand Rapids: Baker Academic, 2004), 53.
10. Richard R. Dunn, *Shaping the Spiritual Life of Students*, 16.

TIMELESS YOUTH MINISTRY

ISBN-13: 978-0-8024-2944-5

Now in paperback, this excellent resource for youth ministry leaders examines afresh what it means to be an adolescent in today's culture and how those who minister to young people can best reach them. Youth ministers Vandegriff and Vukich speak from experience that, while the world of teenagers is in constant change, the eternal message of Christ's love never changes. Topics include a description of adolescence, age characteristics of teens, how self-identity develops, different types of youth work, the purpose and goal of youth ministry, teaching methods, programming, music and worship, principles of counseling youth, and how to set up a counseling session.

1-800-678-8812 • MOODYPUBLISHERS.COM